W9-BAE-603

Famous Men of the
RENAISSANCE &
REFORMATION

by Robert G. Shearer

Greenleaf Press
Lebanon, Tennessee

For Cyndy
the best is yet to be

© Robert G. Shearer, 1996
Published by
Greenleaf Books, LLC
Second Edition, Sixth Printing
2007

All rights reserved. No part of this work may be reproduced or used in any form by any means — graphic, electronic, or mechanical including photocopying, recording, taping or information storage and retrieval systems without written permission from the publisher.

Internet: *www.greenleafpress.com*
3761 Highway 109N, Unit D
Lebanon, Tennessee 37087
615-449-1617

Table of Contents

Author's Preface

This book has been fun to write. It has confirmed for me the wisdom and utility of beginning a study of any historical period with a background in biography. History is after all, about people. And as much as certain modern scholars like to crow about the debunking of the "great man" theory of history, it remains true that certain men (and their ideas) have had more impact and far-reaching influence than others. One needs to understand the important people in order to understand the times. And then one must achieve a deeper understanding of the times in order to understand the important people.

The student who reads these 29 chapters about the lives of 35 or so famous men should come away with a sense of what the periods called the Renaissance and the Reformation were about. It will not, of course, be a complete picture. But it will be a foundation that can be built upon.

I have tried to show the true character and personality of each individual. It has been my conscious intent to avoid painting individuals as heroes or villains. But I have tried to be careful to indicate and include the character flaws of the admirable and even the occasional virtues of the less-than-admirable.

Two criticisms may be leveled at the book from a perusal of the table of contents. First, some will wonder why that group of Reformation Christians known as the Anabaptists are given such prominent coverage. The prominence in this collection (two chapters out of fifteen devoted to the Reformation, three if you include Müntzer) was because of what I believe to have been their unjust obscurity in other treatments of the period. The Anabaptist movement, while always a minority, was much more widespread geographically and more significant politically and theologically than most treatments of the times would at first suggest. The continued attention devoted to rooting them out by authorities throughout this period is but one reason why they deserved a more thorough treatment than they have elsewhere received. Second, some will wonder why there is no discussion of the reforms instituted within the Roman Catholic Church, the so-called Catholic Reformation (or in the older historiography, the Counter Reformation). Although there were genuine reform movements within the church throughout this period, and the "shock troops" of the Catholic Reformation, the Jesuits, were founded in 1540, the true impact of reform within the church was not felt until the second half of the 16th century. I have already resolved, in the next volume of biographies, to devote some chapters to reform with the Roman Catholic Church. The obvious first chapters for the next volume will be Loyola, Philip II, William the Silent, Queen Elizabeth, and Henry of Navarre.

I have tried to show in this volume the continuity between the Renaissance and the Reformation. The revival of learning which characterized the Renaissance led directly to the recovery of the tools and texts that the Reformers used to place the Bible in the language (and hands) of the people. It is an old saw, but true, that "Erasmus laid the egg that Luther hatched."

Almost all of what I have written here is necessarily dependent upon the research of others. I have indicated my main sources in the bibliography at the end. For my introduction to the period and love of history, I owe a great debt to two scholars. First, to Dr. W. Brown Patterson, Dean of the faculty at the University of the South. Dr. Patterson was my undergraduate advisor and sponsor as a history major at Davidson College. Dr. Patterson earned degrees in Renaissance literature, theology, and history and gave me my first introduction to many of the figures I have written about here. More than just an academic advisor, he was also the priest at St. Albans' parish church which I attended. He also helped to officiate at the service in which Cyndy and I were married. Studying the history of the English Reformation while worshipping using the prayer book which was born in that struggle was an exhilarating and humbling experience. It helped me to realize that the issues of the Reformation were still very much alive. My second great scholarly debt is to my graduate advisor, Dr. Lewis W. Spitz of Stanford University, the dean of Luther studies in America. It was Dr. Spitz who guided me through a rigorous program of study and research to familiarize myself with the medieval antecedents of both the Renaissance and the Reformation, and it was his own seminal insight on the relationship between the "three generations of humanists" and the Reformers that helped me to appreciate the connections between those two movements often stereotyped as being at odds. It is no fault of Dr. Spitz's that I never completed my doctoral dissertation, but I hope the fruit of my reading and reflecting on the period in this book is some small consolation.

There are a number of other "famous men" whom I would have liked to include in this work. Selection is always an extremely difficult process. Some were left out for lack of easily accessible resources. Some were left out because their lives overlapped others so much that telling their tale would have been redundant.

In particular I would have liked to have included a chapter on Sir John Hawkwood, the English knight and veteran of the wars in France, who became a mercenary captain in Italy and is honored in Florence by an equestrian statue. I would have liked to have done a chapter on Johannes Reuchlin, the leading German Hebrew scholar and author of a Hebrew grammar used throughout Europe - especially by Luther, Tyndale, and Calvin. I had also thought I would do a chapter on Philip Melanchthon, Luther's learned associate. Melanchthon was Professor of Greek and New Testament at Wittenberg and a great-nephew of Johannes Reuchlin. Unfortunately time, space, and duplication of the events of Luther's life ruled it out. And I had thought I would do a chapter on Martin Bucer, the Dominican monk, admirer of Luther from 1518 on, reformer of Strasburg, mentor of Jean Cauvin, and advocate of toleration towards the Anabaptists. He was forced to flee Strasburg in the 1540's when it was conquered by Charles V, and went to England where he taught Theology at Cambridge and helped Cranmer in the composition of the English Prayer Book. But again, time, space and duplication of the events of Calvin and Cranmer's life seemed to make it better to leave him out.

There is obviously a wealth of additional material that even the beginning student of this period will want to consult. But as an introduction (for students in the elementary grades, high school, and even college) I think this set of biographies may help to intrigue, inform, and begin to form impressions and understanding.

Finally, I must thank my family for their patience as I struggled through the drafting of these chapters. Many of you will know that the work on this book was delayed for almost a year when my wife, Cyndy, suffered with two broken arms from a horseback riding accident. This book was important to me, but I hope readers will understand that taking care of my wife of 19 years ultimately took higher priority. She has, nevertheless been very patient with me and my grumpy moods as I have been bogged down from time to time over the past year. The children also have been very understanding - though they have had to be reminded regularly that Dad's office is not open for casual visits during office hours - especially when I'm writing! Our oldest three have been far enough along in their schooling that they have been able to read some chapters as they were drafted and their feedback has been important. This is a better book for the input and assistance of Cyndy, Jon, Micah, and Jeremy. Paul, Rachel, Hannah, and Jessy gave me lots of hugs and encouragement. As is always the case, the errors, omissions and dumb sentences are mine. The insights and finely worded phrases have usually been suggested to me by others.

I hope that through reading this book, readers will get a better sense of the events that helped to shape the church and an appreciation for the men and women of tremendous ability and often unbelievable courage who were at work in the events of the Renaissance and the Reformation. Let us admire them for their virtues and seek to imitate them, and take caution from their flaws and failures and seek to avoid them. That, after all, is the point of studying history.

— **Rob Shearer**
July 25th, 1996

between the birthdays of Rachel (7/7/1989) and Jessy (8/8/1993) and waiting for the birth of Emily Joy and the arrival of our daughter from China.

Famous Men of the
RENAISSANCE

The Middle Ages were not the "Dark Ages." Yet there had been substantial changes in Europe from 500 to 1300 AD. Rome and her Empire fell. The Germanic tribes moved into the old Roman provinces and established feudal kingdoms. Many of the Roman cities declined in population or were abandoned. Gradually, much of the literature and learning of the classical world was lost and forgotten.

Around 1300, in the towns of northern Italy especially, a group of men began to devote themselves to the recovery and revival of the classical world. Petrarch and his friends were interested above all in recovering the polished, ornate, classical Latin of their hero and model, Cicero. Gradually, the interest in the classical world expanded to include the other ancient languages of Greek and Hebrew. The writers, academics, and artists who shared these interests were called humanists. The name of their party comes from the style of education that they favored — what they called the *studia humanitatis*, or humane studies. They wanted to reform the university program which focused almost exclusively on logic and recognized only a narrow range of authorities, above all, Aristotle. The humanists stressed the importance of rhetoric, the art of speaking and writing persuasively. "Aristotle may define the good, but Plato motivates one to **be** good." In place of Aristotle, the master of logic, they wished to substitute Plato and Cicero, the masters of rhetoric.

The following fourteen individuals are representative of the movement called the Renaissance.

Chapter 1

Petrarch 1304-1374

Petrarch was born at the end of the Middle Ages, in 1304, in the northern Italian city of Florence. His father was a minor government official. Petrarch's time in Florence was short, however. When he was only four, his father wound up on the loosing side of a political quarrel and the family was forced to leave Florence. The family settled in northern Italy where Petrarch's father found work in the service of the Pope as a secretary and notary.

When Petrarch was six, the family was visited by Dante Alighieri, another exile from Florence who had been a friend and ally of Petrarch's father. While in exile Dante wrote one of the most important works of late medieval literature, *The Divine Comedy*. In *The Divine Comedy*, Dante described hell, purgatory, and heaven. As he described each place, Dante passed judgement on both his friends and acquaintances from Florence as well as historical figures from Greece and Rome. He placed each of them in hell, purgatory, or heaven and described their punishment or their reward.

Petrarch grew to admire Dante as he grew older. His father's friend had a strong influence on him, both as a writer and as a moralist. Petrarch shared Dante's admiration for important figures from Greek and Roman history. At an early age, it became clear to Petrarch's parents that their son would have great skill as a writer.

When Petrarch was about 10, political unrest in Rome forced the Pope to move to southern France. Petrarch's father moved his family to France, hoping to continue in the service of the Pope, since he was still forbidden to return to Florence.

When Petrarch was 12, his parents sent him to study law at the University of Montpellier in southern France. He seems to have enjoyed the university at first, but he quickly became disenchanted with the study of law. He later described it as an attempt to master "the art of selling justice." He began to neglect the lectures and courses on law and spent more and more time reading the classics of Roman literature — works by Virgil, Seneca, Julius Caesar, and above all, Cicero.

Eventually, Petrarch's father heard that he was neglecting his studies and paid a visit to his son. He threatened to burn his son's books by Roman authors, but relented when Petrarch burst into tears and begged him not to. Nevertheless, Petrarch's father decided to send his son to another, more prestigious university at Bologna in northern Italy in hopes that he would complete his study of law. Petrarch was 16.

In Bologna, Petrarch and his younger brother Gherardo, studied law for seven years, though Petrarch later called this time "seven wasted years." Once again, he spent much of his time reading his favorite Roman authors. He also practiced writing Latin compositions in imitation of them. His favorite author was Cicero, a Roman lawyer, orator, and Senator whose Latin style was both polished and persuasive. Grudgingly, Petrarch also continued to study law, and learned how to represent clients, draw up contracts, and make presentations to a judge. He still disliked the legal profession intensely.

In 1326, both of Petrarch's parents died. He and his brother left Bologna and returned to their home-in-exile in Avignon, France. He refused to practice law. Instead he took small jobs as a secretary with different officials at the court of the Pope. During this time, he and his brother began to lead the lives of elegant young men-about-town, much concerned with clothes and hair, and admiring the young women of Avignon.

One day, in Avignon, Petrarch had what he described as a "vision." While attending early morning church in April of 1327, he saw a young woman whose beauty immediately captivated him. He believed he had never ever seen anyone so lovely. Her name was Laura. For twenty-one years, she was his inspiration for poetry and prose. The theme of his writings became his eternal, unrequited devotion to Laura.

As time went on, he gradually began to acquire a reputation as one of the most gifted writers in Europe. He wrote romantic poetry, always about Laura, in Italian. In Latin, he wrote summaries of his favorite Roman writers — above all, Cicero — and letter after letter to an ever-widening circle of friends and acquaintances. He was proud of his skill as a writer and was pleased when friends complimented him. The high point of his reputation came in 1341, when his friends in Rome arranged for him to be crowned poet laureate in the ruins of the old Roman capitol. It was a title that had not been in use for almost a thousand years. Petrarch was 37 years old.

At the height of his fame, however, Petrarch became disillusioned with his life. He found that his own fame failed to satisfy him. His love for classical literature and language made him long for the lost power and grandeur of ancient Rome. The contrast between Rome's earlier glory and the current confused state of Italian politics saddened Petrarch deeply. At about the same time, his close relationship with his younger brother changed as well. Gherardo had experienced his own vision of a beautiful woman. But when the "Laura" of his vision suddenly died, he renounced the world, entered a monastery and took a strict vow of silence.

Petrarch sat down, and reflecting on the course of his life, wrote a remarkable book. He called it the *Secretum*. It is set in the form of a dialogue between Petrarch himself, and St. Augustine who acts as a stern father-confessor. Augustine accuses Petrarch of having wasted his life in worldly affections. Petrarch re-examines his love for Laura and concedes that it has not always been pure, but insists that Laura has inspired him to live a better life. Then Augustine accuses Petrarch of caring more for his beloved Roman authors than he does for Christ. To this charge, Petrarch answers:

> "The highest part of my heart is with Christ. When it comes to thinking or speaking of religion, that is, of the highest truth, of true happiness and eternal salvation, I certainly am not a Ciceronian or a Platonist, but a Christian."[1]

In 1348, Laura herself died of the plague. Petrarch was crushed.

Petrarch spent the rest of his life writing and traveling. He devoted much of his time to collecting manuscripts of Roman authors which had been preserved at monasteries in Italy and France. He began to be interested in Greek writers, known to him because his favorite Roman authors quoted them. In particular, he became interested in Plato, since he was quoted often by Cicero. After he acquired a manuscript, in Greek, by Plato, he searched, unsuccessfully, for someone who could help him master classical Greek the way he had mastered classical Latin.

In 1359, while staying in Milan, he was visited by the writer Boccaccio, whom he liked immediately. He and Boccaccio resolved to find a scholar who would translate Homer's epic poems, *The Iliad* and *The Odyssey* in Latin. In this, as with Plato, he was also disappointed. He moved for a time to Venice, then, settled finally in Padua.

Petrarch spent the last fifteen years of his life enjoying his reputation as a poet and champion of classical Latin. He corresponded with friends at the universities and courts of Europe, encouraging them in their study and revival of all things from classical Rome and Greece. He also wrote letters to his ancient heroes, Cicero & Livy. His admiration and longing for the lost grandeur of Rome was intense. To the Roman historian, Livy, he wrote:

> "I would wish either that I had been born in your age, or you in ours. I should thank you, though, that you have so often caused me to forget present evils and have transported me to happier times. As I read, I seem to be living amidst Scipio, Brutus, and Cato. It is with these men that I live at such times, and not with the thievish company of today, among whom I was born under an evil star."[2]

Towards the end of his life, he was visited by four young scholars from the local university who were not very appreciative of his status as a classical scholar. They shocked him with their curt dismissal of both Paul and Augustine. They thought Aristotle, and his Arab commentator, Averroes, the only writers worth reading and studying. In response, he wrote a treatise entitled, *On His Own Ignorance and that of Many Others*. In it he was sharply critical of the teaching of Aristotle in the universities. He disputed the medieval notion that Aristotle was the greatest of the philosophers. He argued for the favorite philosopher of his Roman heroes, Plato. Petrarch argued that although Aristotle might be preferred by a greater number of authors, Plato is preferred by the greater men.

Finally, on a warm summer morning in July of 1374, the day before his seventieth birthday, Petrarch's servants came in to find him slumped over at his desk. He had been working on his *Life of Julius Caesar*, written in classical Latin, when he died.

Some years before his death he had written a letter to those who would read about him after his death:

"Francesco Petrarca to Posterity, Greeting.

Perhaps you will have heard somewhat about me. Perhaps, too, you will wish to know what sort of man I was. Youth ensnared me; early manhood carried me away; but old age corrected me, and by experience taught me the truth of which I had read so often — that youth and pleasures are vanity. I devoted myself to a knowledge of antiquity, for this age of ours I have always found distasteful, so that, had it not been for the love of those dear to me, I should have preferred to have been born in any other. And so I strove to forget the present and join myself in spirit with the past."[3]

Sonnet 231

Life hurries on, a frantic refugee,

And Death, with great forced marches, follows fast,

And all the present leagues with all the past

And all the future to make war on me.

Anticipation joins to memory

To search my soul with daggers; and at last,

Did not damnation set me so aghast,

I'd put an end to thinking and be free.

The few glad moments that my heart has known

Return to me; then I foresee in dread

The winds upgathering against my ways,

Storm in the harbor, and the pilot prone,

The mast and rigging down; and dark and dead

The lovely lights whereon I used to gaze.

— **(translated by Morris Bishop)**[4]

Chapter **2**

Giotto 1267-1336

G iotto was born in 1267, in a small village about 14 miles from Florence. His parents were peasant farmers, and Giotto grew up accustomed to all the chores of a farming family. But Giotto was always interested in more than just farming. He was always fascinated with nature — plants, animals, & scenic views — and he was always drawing pictures of what he saw.

When Giotto was about 10, his father made him responsible for the care of a flock of sheep. Since the sheep were relatively self-sufficient, Giotto had lots of free time for his favorite activity — drawing. He drew on flat rocks with pieces of charcoal. He drew with sticks in the dirt and sand. One day, while Giotto was making a sketch of one of his sheep on a flat rock, a passing traveler stopped to admire his work, impressed with the realistic, lifelike details of Giotto's sketch. The traveler was one of the most famous artists of his day, Cimabue. He introduced himself to Giotto and asked if he would like to come and work with him in his workshop in Florence. Giotto replied, "If my father will allow it, I would willingly come and work with you." Giotto's father quickly gave his consent.

In Florence, Giotto quickly became Cimabue's star pupil. It was not long before the skill of the pupil equaled and then exceeded his teacher. A story from Giotto's apprenticeship illustrates how vivid, lifelike, and natural his painting was. One day, when Cimabue left the workshop, Giotto went to a portrait just finished by his master and painted a fly on the nose of the figure. When Cimabue returned to the workshop, he tried several times to shoo the fly away with his hand before he realized that his pupil had played a prank on him.

Madonna *by Cimabue*

Madonna *by Giotto*

St. Francis Gives His Cloak
to a Stranger *by Giotto*

After he reached his 20's, Giotto began to receive independent commissions to paint frescos and portraits. These were almost always of scenes described in the Bible, or from the lives of Christian saints. They usually were intended to decorate churches or monasteries. The churches of Florence each had many chapels, many paid for by leading families. Each of these families wanted their chapel to have the most impressive artwork. Giotto was much in demand.

With each commission he completed, his reputation grew. Word reached him from the northern Italian town of Assisi. The Vicar General of the Franciscans had a special commission for him. The head of the Franciscans wished Giotto to paint the life of St. Francis, 32 panels in all, on both walls of the central sanctuary of the Franciscan orders' mother church. This work occupied Giotto for several years, but when he was finished, the panels were masterpieces. In these panels, Giotto showed that he had mastered the realistic portrayal of human forms in natural settings. The dramatic presentation of the various incidents of the life of St. Francis is vivid and arresting. As soon as they were completed, young painters and admirers began flocking to Assisi to admire them. They are still coming, 700 years later!

Word of his accomplishments reached the Pope in Rome, who was looking for an artist to execute several paintings at the cathedral of St. Peter. Pope Boniface VIII dispatched an emissary to Florence to make inquiries concerning Giotto as well as a number of other prominent artists. He interviewed patrons, inspected completed paintings, and collected drawings from each artist to take back to Rome so the Pope could make his final selection. When he asked Giotto for a small sketch to take back to Rome so that the Pope could evaluate his work, Giotto had an unusual response. He took a sheet of paper and a brush dipped in red paint and with one stroke painted a complete circle. Handing the sheet to the emissary, he said "Here is your drawing. Send it along with the others and you will see whether or not it will be understood."

When the Pope and his advisors heard the emissary's description of how Giotto had painted the circle before them with one stroke, they realized just how far Giotto surpassed all the other painters of his time in skill. The Pope invited Giotto to Rome. There he executed a number of frescoes and paintings in St. Peter's and for the Pope's residence, though few have survived. After a number of years in Rome, the Pope died and Giotto's commissions were not renewed by his successor. He traveled briefly to Naples in southern Italy and then spent time painting commissions in churches in Rimini, Ravenna, Arezzo, and Padua.

In 1334, Giotto, now in his 60's, was summoned to Florence and offered the prestigious position as the head of the Florence Cathedral workshop. Here he was given charge of the planning for the grand new cathedral, its bell tower, and all the artwork that would adorn the interior and exterior. The work continued long after Giotto's death, but his design and plan for the bell tower (*Campanille*) have long been admired. The bell tower uses three different shades of marble to highlight and decorate its vertical lines. Giotto's original plan seems to have called for a four-sided pyramid to be constructed at the top of the square building, but this was never completed.

Giotto's Belltower, Florence, Italy

Giotto's tenure in Florence did not last long. He died in 1336 and was buried in one of the churches in Florence. Succeeding generations of artists in Europe were inspired by him and admired his work. Giorgio Vasari, in his Lives of the Artists describes him as "born to give birth to the art of painting."

Over a hundred years after his death, the Medici family in Florence commissioned a marble bust of Giotto and had it installed in the church of Santa Maria del Fiore, with the following inscription:

"I am that man by whose deeds painting was raised from the dead, my hand as ready as it was sure. My art lacked nothing that nature herself did not also lack. No one has painted anything better or more completely than I did. Do you admire a beautiful tower resounding with sacred sound? By my design this tower reached for the stars. But I am Giotto, why cite such deeds? My name alone has inspired many a poem."[5]

Lamentation over the Dead Christ *by Giotto*

Chapter 3

Filippo Brunelleschi 1377-1446 and Donatello 1386-1466

T owards the end of the Middle Ages, the city of Florence, in northern Italy, acquired an excellent reputation for the fine quality of the cloth it produced. Skilled craftsmen in Florence bought wool from shepherds in the northern Italian countryside and turned it into yarn and then wove it into beautiful wool cloth. Merchants sent out by the city bought fine silk and cotton in the Middle East and brought it back where it was dyed and finished for export all over Europe.

As Florence's fame and prosperity grew, she began to send representatives farther and farther away to buy raw materials for her cloth trade and to sell the fine finished goods. These traveling merchants became very wealthy. In order to make their trade easier, they also invented many of the features of modern banking — especially the ability to deposit money with an office in one city and withdraw it from an office of the same bank in another city. By 1300, the merchants and bankers of Florence were among the richest people in Europe. Florence itself, with a population of about 100,000 was the largest city in Europe.

In 1290, the leading citizens of Florence, led by the officers of the wool guild, decided that the city needed a new and larger cathedral. They wished to show their gratitude to God who had blessed them and caused them to prosper. They also wished for a large cathedral which would show the rest of northern Italy just how prosperous Florence was. The building they planned was designed to be the largest church in Europe. It eventually took almost 200 years to finish. The old cathedral was torn down and the foundations

The Duomo in Florence

laid for the new structure on a truly grand scale. The plans called for a central dome which would span an open vault more than 130 feet across above the altar where the two wings of the church nave crossed. By 1400 they were ready to start the dome. But no one knew how to build such a large, free standing structure. No dome on this scale had ever been built. The priors of the city (the elected leaders of the city) announced a competition to select the man who would oversee the building of the dome. The man who successfully completed the building of the dome would be hailed as the greatest architect of Europe.

Filippo Brunelleschi was born in 1377 to a wealthy family of Florence. His father was a notary — similar to a modern lawyer. He drafted contracts and carried on correspondence for his employer with employees and partners in cities all across Europe. Filippo's father trained him in his own profession and although Filippo was quite bright and clever with words, his father's profession did not appeal to him. Filippo liked to work with his hands. He liked to draw. He liked to analyze anything mechanical in order to understand how it worked. Bowing to his son's natural inclinations, Filippo's father apprenticed him to a goldsmith. Filippo very quickly mastered the art of working with gold and silver and precious stones. From there he progressed to designing and building fine and beautiful clocks.

Then, while still in his early 20's, Filippo decided he wished to master the art of sculpture. He became close friends with a young teen-ager named Donatello, already considered the most talented sculptor in Florence. Donatello shared what he had already learned about sculpture with his friend Filippo. Together they studied the examples of ancient Greek and Roman sculpture which had been brought to Florence.

One day, Donatello took his friend Filippo to the Church of Santa Croce in Florence to admire a wooden crucifix which he had just completed. Filippo admired the craftsmanship of his friend, but criticized the design. "The figure you have carved is not that of Jesus, the son of God. It looks more like a peasant," he said. Donatello was cross and snapped that Filippo ought to "take some wood and make one yourself." Filippo made no reply but later began

14

work on a crucifix of his own. Some weeks later, he met Donatello in the market. Giving him the groceries he had bought, he asked Donatello to take them to his home and he would follow shortly, after he had made a few more purchases. When Donatello entered the house, he was stunned by the finished crucifix which Filippo had left in a prominent place in the entryway. He stood in the doorway, staring at the carved figure, and so forgot himself, that he dropped the milk, eggs, and cheese he had been carrying for Filippo in his apron. When Filippo arrived a few moments later, he found Donatello still transfixed, staring at the crucifix, with the smashed eggs and spilled groceries at his feet. "Now how can we have lunch, since you've spilled everything?" asked Filippo. "I've had enough," said Donatello. "It is for you to make Christs, and for me to make peasants!"

Shortly after this, the city officials decided to commission new bronze doors for the baptistery. The baptistery was a small, separate building, sort of a chapel in which baptisms were conducted — it stands next to the cathedral in Florence. They asked Filippo, Donatello, and another young man, named Lorenzo Ghiberti (who was to be Filippo's lifelong rival) to each cast a single bronze panel on the same theme, "the sacrifice of Isaac." Ghiberti was 23, Filippo was 24, and Donatello was 15. These young men had already acquired reputations as the most gifted artists in Florence.

When each had finished their panels, they were all brought to the city hall to be placed together and judged. When the panels were revealed, Filippo and Donatello both agreed that Ghiberti's panel showed the best design and the best execution. Together, they persuaded the city council to award the contract for the doors of the baptistery to Ghiberti. The council asked both Donatello and Filippo to assist Ghiberti in the project, but they both declined (although later, both Donatello and Filippo helped Lorenzo in polishing and finishing the doors).

Filippo later said he had refused because he wished to find some craft or skill in which he could be the very best — not second-best. He persuaded Donatello to accompany him to Rome so that they might study further the art, sculpture, and architecture of the ancient Romans. He sold a farm which had been given him by his father, and taking the proceeds with him moved to Rome, where he stayed for six years.

The ruins of classical Rome fascinated and amazed Filippo. No other city in Europe had buildings like these! The Romans had a wealth of knowledge about architecture and construction that builders in the Middle Ages had forgotten. Filippo set out to make a systematic study of all the buildings of the ancients. He and Donatello sketched each building, wall, and arch from a variety of angles. They measured the dimensions of foundations meticulously. Where foundations had been partially buried, they took picks and shovels and dug them out. The people of Rome didn't quite know what to make of these two young men who spent every day among the ruins.

After a year or so, Donatello returned to Florence, but Filippo stayed in Rome. As he continued to study the ancient buildings, he decided that he would devote himself to a revival of the art of architecture. At some point, he resolved that, by studying the art of the Romans, he would find the solution to the problem of completing the dome of the cathedral in Florence.

Filippo's studies in Rome had another important effect. By carefully comparing the measurements that he and Donatello had made with the sketches they had done of the appearances of the ancient buildings, Filippo was able to work out a precise understanding of the technique of perspective. The use of perspective in drawing is what makes objects farther away appear smaller and objects closer appear larger. Filippo realized that square objects, with parallel lines in three dimensions appear to have lines that converge on the horizon when sketched in two dimensions. His measurements and skills at geometry allowed him to use perspective in his drawings in a way that produces a startling realism.

In 1407 Filippo returned to Florence. He was now 30 years old. He shared with Donatello and other artists his discoveries on perspective and they quickly learned and adopted his technique. He spent some time assisting Ghiberti in the completion of the bronze panels for the Baptistery doors. But again and again, he returned to the site of the unfinished cathedral in the center of Florence and studied the unfinished, open space, which waited for a dome. He talked to carpenters and stonemasons, all the while formulating his plan. He spent time working on additions being made to several of the smaller churches in Florence, and perfected the art of completing a vaulted, domed ceiling without costly supporting wood framework.

In 1420, the priors announced that they would award the commission for completing the dome of the cathedral to whichever architect demonstrated that he possessed the best technique and judgement for completing the work. Many foreign engineers and architects were invited by Florentine merchants and bankers throughout Europe to come to Florence to compete for the job. When all had assembled, the priors invited each one to present his ideas. All sorts of wild ideas were put forward. One engineer proposed filling the cathedral in with dirt to support the arches of the dome while they were being built. Asked how he would go about removing the dirt when the job was finished, the imaginative engineer suggested that bags of valuable coins should be placed inside the dirt mound. Then the public would be invited to remove the dirt, with permission to keep whatever coins they found.

Only Filippo proposed that the dome could be built without any supporting framework, pillars, or dirt. The priors were skeptical. The other engineers and architects scoffed. The priors were not convinced by Filippo's arguments. The rival engineers and architects demanded that Filippo produce the model of his proposed dome which they knew he had been working on in secret to show how he planned to build it. Filippo refused. Filippo objected to his competitors that once he showed them how he planned to build the dome, they would all steal his carefully thought out plans. Finally, Filippo produced an egg and announced that whoever could stand the egg upright on a marble slab should be given the job of building the dome. Each of the other masters tried in turn, but none of them could make the egg stand up. Finally, they asked Filippo if he could do it. Filippo took the egg and tapped the larger end against the marble, cracking and partially collapsing it. He then stood the egg upright on its cracked base. The other artisans began to complain loudly that any of them could have done the same thing. Filippo laughed and replied, "Yes you could, **AFTER**

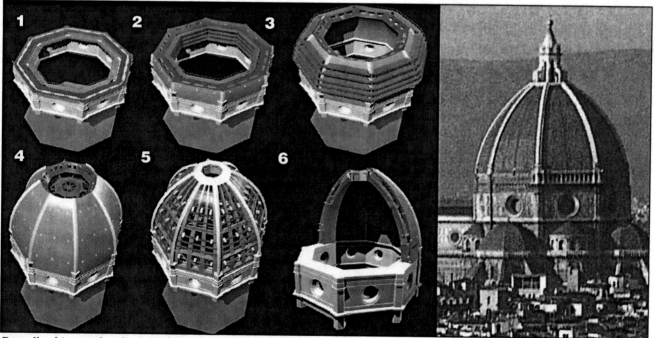

Brunelleschi started with scaffolding around the inside of the dome (fig. 1); as the walls were built upwards the inner scaffolding supported the inward-sloping walls and scaffolding was added on the outside (figs. 2 & 3); as the dome progressed, the scaffolding was able to span the narrowed distance within the inner shell (fig. 4); Fig. 5 shows the interior structure of the dome including the vertical ribs and six horizontal iron chains which strengthened the structure. The dome is complete except for the lantern; Fig. 6 is a cutaway showing the double-shell construction of the dome. On the right is a photograph of the completed dome.

you had seen it done. Just as, **AFTER** you have seen my model, you will all know how to build the dome." The priors awarded Filippo the contract.

For sixteen years, Filippo directed the work on the dome. He was meticulous in supervising all the details of construction. He designed and had constructed all the frames and scaffolding and hoists needed to bring the material up for the construction of the dome. When he noticed how much time was lost during the break for the mid-day meal, he had several wooden structures constructed on top of the cathedral walls with complete kitchens where the workmen could get a hot meal and purchase wine and other refreshments. Filippo went to the kiln where the bricks were manufactured to inspect the clay. He went to the quarry where stones were being prepared to make sure they were not cracked. He gave the masons and stone-cutters detailed models of how each joint and fitting were to be constructed.

About 1430, impressed with his success in guiding the construction of the dome, Filippo was approached by the leading (and wealthiest) citizen of Florence, Cosimo de' Medici. Cosimo asked Filippo to supervise the completion of a church which Cosimo's father had begun. Filippo revised the building plans and took over the construction. His good friend Donatello was commissioned to decorate the interior of the church with stuccoes, carvings, and bronze panels on the doors. Cosimo was so pleased with Filippo's work on the church that he next commissioned him to design and construct a grand home for the Medici family.

From then on, to the end of his life, there was no shortage of building projects for Filippo to work on. One of his last designs was for the cupola which was to be built on top of the dome over the cathedral. Filippo completed the design before his death, but the cupola itself was not finished until 1482, thirty-six years after he died, in 1446.

After he died, the Florentine historian Giorgio Vasari described Brunelleschi in the following way:

> "Nature has created many men who are small and insignificant in appearance but who are endowed with spirits so full of greatness and hearts of such boundless courage that they have no peace until they undertake difficult and almost impossible tasks and bring them to completion, to the astonishment of those who witness them."[6]

Chapter *4*

Lorenzo Valla 1407-1457

About the time Donatello was studying the ruins of ancient Rome, Lorenzo Valla was born there. He was quickly recognized as a prodigy. He was born in Rome in 1407 and mastered classical Latin at an early age. He studied Petrarch's letters and shared Petrarch's admiration for Cicero. After mastering the complexities of classical Latin, he turned his attention to another ancient language, Greek. This was somewhat unusual for the time, because the Greek language was largely unknown in Europe, being almost as difficult for scholars then as Egyptian hieroglyphics would be centuries later. But Valla persisted, and by seeking out the Greek-speaking representatives of the Eastern Emperor and the patriarch of Constantinople, he managed to master the Greek language. He became so accomplished in Greek translation and composition that he was sought after by the Pope and prominent Cardinals in their dealings with the Byzantine (or Eastern Roman) Empire.

Valla wrote a number of essays which contributed to his fame as a learned scholar. One of his first compositions was a dialogue between a Stoic, a Christian and an Epicurean titled, *Concerning the True Good*. His reputation as a scholar of classical Latin was established with a handbook he published in 1444 called *Elegances of the Latin Language*. He discussed in detail the rhetorical art of speaking and writing persuasively using the classical, Ciceronian Latin style. A great deal of the work was devoted to the art of choosing exactly the right word. Although two words may be synonyms, they often carry different connotations. For example, "order" and "series" both mean a succession of things, but "order" implies a plan and "series" does not. For several generations, Valla's book was the style guide for all serious writers of classical Latin.

Valla also used his knowledge of the classics to write several philosophical works. One of the most important was his essay, *On Free Will*. In this essay he argued strongly that predestination and free will do not contradict each other, nor does God's knowledge of the future mean that human beings are not free. He had to admit that there were some concepts that troubled him, but concluded that "We stand by faith, not by the probabilities of reason."

Perhaps Valla's most important work was his *Annotations to the New Testament* in which he examined the style of Jerome's translation of the New Testament into Latin. Because of his skill with the Greek language he was able to correct a number of misreadings and mistakes which Jerome had made.

In 1440 Valla wrote his most sensational work entitled *The False "Donation of Constantine."* This was an analysis of the document used by the Pope to justify his secular authority over the city of Rome and the territory in central Italy known as the Papal States. This document, known as *The Donation of Constantine*, was supposed to be a grant of the city of Rome (and outlying provinces) made to Pope Sylvester by the Emperor Constantine the Great (the first Christian Emperor) when he moved the capitol of the Empire to Constantinople in 330 A.D.

Valla analyzed the document and criticized it because it did not seem likely that an Emperor in 300 A.D. would have made such a grant, or that the Pope would have accepted it. But then Valla went further. By a close analysis of the words and style used in the document, he showed that it could not have been written in 330 A.D. but was a forgery — created 500 years AFTER Constantine had left Rome, most likely around 800 A.D.

Eighty years later, a German monk you will read about later in this book said that Valla and Wyclif were the two men who most influenced his ideas about the condition of the church and the authority of the papacy.

Chapter **5**

Cosimo de' Medici 1389-1464

I n the chapter on Filippo Brunelleschi, we saw how Florence had prospered because of its cloth trade. As the cloth merchants ranged over Europe and the Mediterranean they developed most of the features of modern branch banking in order to carry on their trading. Many of the cloth merchants became quite wealthy and over time their activities as bankers became more profitable than the cloth trade.

The government of Florence was organized around the guilds of the various professions. There were 21 guilds in all. The most important ones were the lawyers, wool merchants, silk merchants, cloth merchants, bankers, fur merchants, and finally, the sellers of spices, dyes, and medicines. Florence was governed by a council, which was supposed to be selected at random from all eligible members of the twenty-one guilds. Six members of the council came from the seven prominent guilds. Two came from the other fourteen guilds. The ninth member of the council was its most important, called the *Gonfaloniere*. The *Gonfaloniere* led the council and thus the city. The members of the council, including the *Gonfaloniere*, were supposed to be chosen at random from among all eligible guild members. In practice however, the wealthiest families of Florence managed to ensure that only the names of their allies and supporters made their way into the leather bags from which the random selections were made.

One of the wealthiest families to emerge from the cloth trade and international banking was the Medici of Florence. By 1400, the Medici had become the wealthiest of a whole class of prosperous merchants in Florence. Florence, itself, was not the largest city in Europe (London, Paris, Rome, even Venice had a larger population), but it was one of the richest. There were other prosperous families in Florence — the Alberti, the Ricci, and the Spini — but the Medici had an advantage that they did not. For the Medici had become the bankers for the Pope.

In the early 1400's, the head of the Medici family was named Cosimo. Born in 1389, Cosimo received a classical education at a monastery school in Florence. Studying with teachers who were devoted followers of both Dante and Petrarch, Cosimo acquired a deep respect for classical learning and classical ideals. He began to collect classical manuscripts of Greek and Roman authors at an early age. But his education was also practical. His father and uncles taught him the family banking business — in which he soon showed great skill. As a young man in his 20's, Cosimo spent three years managing the family's banking business in Rome.

The Medici were very active in the politics of Florence, but they almost always remained in the background. They were the wealthiest family in the city, but Cosimo's father realized that many could easily become envious of their wealth and power if it were too prominently displayed. On his deathbed, he advised his son Cosimo:

> "Do not appear to give advice, but put your views forward discreetly in con-
> versation. Be wary of going to the *Palazzo della Signoria* [the town hall];
> wait to be summoned, and when you are summoned, do what you are asked
> to do, and never display any pride should you receive a lot of votes... avoid
> litigation and political controversy, and always keep out of the public eye..."[7]

Soon after his father's death, Cosimo saw the wisdom of that advice. His rivals began to stir up trouble and used rumors of the great wealth of the Medici to arouse envy and resentment. In 1433, Cosimo's rivals managed to elect a council that was composed of their allies and Cosimo's enemies. Cosimo was arrested and for a time it looked as if he might be executed on trumped up charges of conspiring with enemies of the Florentine Republic. Some skillful political maneuvering and a few well-placed bribes managed to reduce the sentence to banishment for Cosimo and other prominent members of the Medici family.

Almost exactly one year later, in 1434, Cosimo, with the assistance of the Pope, engineered a reversal of his political fortunes. A new council was elected, the sentence of banishment on the Medici was revoked, and this time it was the rivals of the Medici who were banished. For the next 30 years, Cosimo managed political affairs in Florence. During that time he worked most often behind the scenes, as inconspicuous as possible. Only three times during the 30 year period did he hold the office of Gonfaloniere. As one of his friends observed, "whenever he wished to achieve something, he saw to it, in order to escape envy as much as possible, that the initiative appeared to come from others and not from him." A contemporary historian observed, "He had a reputation such as probably no private citizen has ever enjoyed from the fall of Rome to our own day."

In 1439, Cosimo and Florence played host to one of the most important church conferences in several centuries — a general council of the Greek Orthodox and Roman Catholic churches. The council was attended by Bishops, Archbishops, and Cardinals from all the important cities of Europe and the Mediterranean and the East. After all the delegates had assembled in Ferrara in 1438, they accepted an invitation from Cosimo d'Medici to move the council to Florence in 1439. Attending the council were not only the Bishops, but the Pope, the Patriarch of Constantinople, and the Eastern Roman Emperor himself.

The council had been called at the insistence of the Eastern Roman Emperor. His kingdom had shrunk in the last 30 years and the Ottoman Turks were now threatening the city of Constantinople itself. The Eastern Emperor wished desperately for military assistance from the Roman Catholic west. He hoped the council would come to an agreement on reunification between the eastern and western churches.

After some months of delay, an agreement was reached. It was announced in Latin by Cardinal Cesarini and by Archbishop Bessarion in Greek. Then the Italian cardinal and the Greek archbishop embraced each other and, joined by all the other delegates and the Eastern Emperor, they knelt before the Pope. But the celebrations were premature. The agreement reached in Florence was denounced widely and strongly by Greek Orthodox church leaders when they learned its terms, and the promised military assistance from the West never materialized. Fourteen years later, in 1453, the last Eastern Emperor died in battle as the Turks breached the walls of Constantinople and overran the city.

There were lasting effects from the council in Florence. Several of the Greek scholars who had traveled with the Eastern Emperor were persuaded to remain in Florence and continue their instruction in classical Greek and on the study of Plato — who had long been overshadowed in the medieval universities by his pupil, Aristotle. Cosimo was so taken with Plato that he founded a Platonic Academy in Florence and installed a promising young student, Marsilio Ficino as its head. For years, Cosimo paid all of the expenses of the academy out of his own pocket — enabling Ficino to devote his time to his studies and to translate all of Plato's writings into Latin. But Cosimo's support was not simply financial. He often met with Ficino and they would discuss Plato and questions of philosophy for hours at a time.

In addition to supporting the Platonic Academy, Cosimo spent huge sums acquiring manuscripts for his library. Agents of the Medici banks all through Europe were constantly on the lookout for manuscripts of Greek or Latin authors. Eventually, Cosimo owned thousands.

Cosimo was also a patron of the arts. His father had been one of the priors of the cathedral who had commissioned Ghiberti to cast the bronze doors for the baptistery. Cosimo continued his support for the construction of the cathedral and the completion of its dome, but he lavished most of his church-building support on the Dominican monastery of San Marco. The prior of the monastery became a close friend of Cosimo's. Over the course of thirty years, Cosimo paid for the monastery to be almost completely rebuilt — at a fantastic cost. When the monks once protested that he was giving too much, Cosimo replied, "Never shall I be able to give God enough to set him down in my books as a debtor." Cosimo asked his friend the prior to set aside one of the monk's cells for his own use and he often spent time in the monastery in reflection.

In addition to the money that Cosimo spent on rebuilding the Dominican monastery, he also commissioned a wonderful series of frescoes to adorn the walls of each monk's cell as well as the halls and meeting rooms of the monastery. These frescoes were painted by a monk who became known as Fra Angelico — "Brother Angel." He was a small and saintly friar, who had been encouraged by Cosimo to use his skill in painting to depict scenes from the life of Christ. Cosimo was very interested in all of his paintings. He talked with Fra Angelico about the details and composition of each fresco. For the Chapter House (where all of the monks assembled for worship and for official meetings),

Cosimo and Fra Angelico decided that the walls should be decorated with a fresco depicting *The Crucifixion*.

Every morning before he began work on *The Crucifixion*, Fra Angelico would kneel in prayer. Each day, as he worked on his portrayal of Christ's suffering on the Cross, he would be so overcome with emotion that tears would pour down his cheeks. He was a man of simplicity, modesty and holiness, exemplifying the monastic ideal in a way which few other monks did. It is said that his fellow friars never saw him angry.

For his own cell in the monastery, Cosimo asked Fra Angelico to paint the *Adoration of the Magi* so as to have the example of the kings laying down their crowns at the manger always before him.

The Adoration of the Magi by Fra Angelico
Painted for Cosimo's cell at San Marco

Cosimo was also the patron of several other important artists of the Renaissance — none of them with so admirable a character as Fra Angelico, but gifted painters none-the-less. Donatello (the friend of Brunelleschi) was a special favorite of Cosimo as was Fra Filippo Lippi. Lippi was another monk who was a brilliant painter. But his life had almost none of the admirable qualities of Fra Angelico. He was a liar, a cheat and a fraud — as well as being a notorious chaser of women! His paintings, though, were among the most beautiful of the Renaissance. He trained a generation of artists in his workshop in Florence, among them, one important young artist named Botticelli. Cosimo winced at many of Lippi's escapades. He frequently chastised the artist for his immoral behavior and tried to reform him, but continued to

Madonna by Fra Filippo Lippi

support him with gifts and commissions because of his talent as an artist.

Finally, a word should be said about Cosimo's devotion to his grandchildren. No matter how busy Cosimo was — or how important the business might seem — Cosimo always had time for his grandchildren. One story will suffice to illustrate his devotion to them. One day, Cosimo was discussing some important matters with a delegation from another city when one of his grandchildren came into the room and interrupted the conference to ask his grandfather to make him a whistle. The meeting was immediately adjourned and Cosimo set to work. When one of the delegation complained the next day, Cosimo replied, "Oh my lords, are you not also fathers and grandfathers? You must not be surprised that I should have made a whistle. It's a good thing that the boy didn't ask me to play it for him; because I would have done that too."

Cosimo died in 1464, at the age of 76. After his death, the council of Florence conferred on him the title *Pater Patriae*, father of his country.

The Adoration of the Magi *by Botticelli*
According to Vasari, this is almost a Medici family portrait. Cosimo is kneeling in the center on the steps at the feet of the Christ child. His son, Piero is kneeling in the center at the bottom of the steps. Piero's elder son, Lorenzo is standing, on the far left, holding a sword. Piero's younger son, Giuliano, is kneeling, immediately to his right. Botticelli placed himself at the far right of the painting, returning the gaze of the viewer.

Chapter 6

Lorenzo de' Medici 1449-1492

When Cosimo died in 1464, his eldest son, Piero then aged 48 succeeded him as head of the family. After the death of Cosimo, Piero faced the hostility of a number of rival families who had always disliked the Medici. These rival families, believing Piero to be a weaker man than his father, plotted to remove the Medici from all political influence in Florence. But they underestimated Piero. Piero discovered, countered, and defeated the schemes of his rivals. Whether confronted with internal political revolt or external threats from rival cities, he rose to the occasion, marshaled his forces, and defeated his enemies. But Piero's health was not strong. He had been ill for many years. Five years after his father's death, Piero died and was buried near Cosimo, his father, in the Church of San Lorenzo.

He left behind a wife and five children — two sons and three daughters. His wife, Lucrezia Tornabuoni, was an admired and accomplished woman. She had received an education in classical languages herself and was an accomplished poet who wrote hymns and translated sections of the Bible into verse. She was also a loving wife and mother, adored by her husband and her children, and by her father-in-law, Cosimo de' Medici himself.

Their eldest son was named Lorenzo and his younger brother was Giuliano. Lorenzo had been 15, and Giuliano 11 when their grandfather died. Now at 20 and 16, their father was dead also, and Lorenzo was catapulted to a position as head of the Medici family. He was exceptionally well prepared for the task.

As a youth, Lorenzo had been given an education by some of the most learned men of Italy. One of his tutors had been Marsilio Ficino, who had been commissioned by Cosimo to translate the works of Plato from Greek into Latin. From his tutors, Lorenzo learned the history of the ancient civilizations of Greece and Rome. He learned to compose orations and poetry in the complicated classical Latin style of Cicero. By the time Lorenzo was 15, he was already an accomplished poet. He acquired a love of learning and classical antiquity which lasted his entire lifetime.

His father had noticed Lorenzo's remarkable skills even when his son was still quite young. Piero began to send Lorenzo on diplomatic missions while he was still 15 years old. Lorenzo traveled as the official representative of Florence (and the Medici family) on missions to Pisa, Milan, Bologna, Venice, Ferrara, Naples, and Rome.

When Lorenzo turned 19, his parents decided that it was time for him to marry. To further the family interests, they decided to break with tradition and look for a wife outside the other wealthy families of Florence. Since the Medici bank in Rome (which handled the banking transactions of the Popes) was the most important branch of the family banks, it seemed only natural to find Lorenzo a bride from among the powerful families of Rome. Clarice Orsini was the daughter of one of the two most important families in Rome. The Orsini family had been important in Roman and Papal politics since the 12th century. Three medieval popes had come from the Orsini family (Celestine III, Nicolas III, and Benedict XII) and they were always influential in the College of Cardinals.

To celebrate Lorenzo's engagement, his mother and father hosted an outdoor festival in the Piazza Santa Croce in February of 1469. Lorenzo and a dozen of his friends took part in a tournament of knights. Lorenzo and the cream of Florentine youth were all arrayed in glittering costumes and elaborate suits of armor and helmets for the contest. Spectators crowded onto roofs and balconies around the Piazza to watch the competition. Lorenzo competed in all the events, riding a white stallion which had been sent as a gift from the King of Naples. Gifts from other Italian rulers included a polished suit of armor from the Duke of Milan and another stallion sent by the Duke of Ferrara. Lorenzo, of course, was awarded first prize in the tournament by the judges.

Four months later, Clarice Orsini arrived from Rome for the wedding. For over a week Florence and the Medici celebrated with parties and receptions. Six months later,

Lorenzo's father Piero died. Even though he was not yet 21 and had been married for less than six months, Lorenzo was now the head of the Medici family and the leading citizen of Florence.

The opponents of the Medici family, who had been defeated by Piero, saw in Lorenzo's youth weakness that could be exploited. The exiled opponents assembled a small army of mercenaries and seized a small town on the edge of the Republic of Florence's territory. But Lorenzo and the Signoria acted quickly and decisively. They sent a military force of their own and stormed the city, scattering the enemies of the Medici.

Lorenzo, like his father and grandfather, held no title or office of his own. He was not Duke of Florence. Florence was a republic and continued to be ruled by elected representatives of the 21 guilds. Although he had no special status or title, everyone knew that Lorenzo de' Medici was Florence's leading citizen.

The enemies of the Medici never gave up their goal of removing the Medici from political power in Florence. Some of them, made bitter by their defeats by Cosimo, Piero and Lorenzo, wanted to see the Medici family destroyed. In 1475 the enemies of the Medici began to plot once again. This time they had a powerful ally — the Pope, himself.

Why Pope Sixtus IV hated the Medici is not easy to explain. It may have been partly because the Medici bank had been reluctant to loan him the large sums of money he wished to spend acquiring towns and territory for his nephews. It may have been partly that the Pope perceived Lorenzo's alliance of Northern Italian cities (Florence, Milan, and Venice) to be directed against Rome. It was probably partly that the Pope's family had long been rivals to the family of Lorenzo's wife, Clarice Orsini.

The Medici had other enemies. In 1474, the Pope appointed one Francesco Salviati as Archbishop of Pisa. But Pisa was part of the territory of the Florentine Republic, and the Republic had an agreement with the Pope that no appointments would be made in their territory without its approval. The Signoria of Florence therefore refused to permit Salviati to come to Pisa and assume his office. For three years, Salviati waited in Rome, blaming the Medici of Florence for his plight.

In January 1477, Salviati, Girolamo Riario (one of the Pope's nephews), and Francesco de Pazzi, manager of the Rome branch of the Pazzi family bank (with its home office in Florence) met together in Rome. Riario's ambition was to enlarge the territory he controlled by annexing territory from the Florentine Republic. Francesco Pazzi thought that it was high time that the Medici family in Florence be destroyed and his own family placed in control of the Republic. And Salviati was embittered over the refusal of the Signoria of Florence to allow him to assume his position as Bishop of Pisa.

For a year they plotted, gaining the approval of Pope Sixtus himself for their plans. In April of 1478 they struck. At Sunday Mass in the great Cathedral (the Duomo) of Florence, at the moment the church bells sounded, the band of assassins (there were at least four) pulled daggers and attacked both Giuliano and Lorenzo. Giuliano was killed, but Lorenzo was only wounded. Lorenzo's friends immediately bustled him out of the Cathedral and back to the Medici Palace. When word spread throughout Florence of what the conspirators had done, the conspiracy quickly collapsed. The people of Florence took immediate revenge on the Pazzi family and all of the conspirators. Salviati and Francesco Pazzi were both hanged from the overhanging roof of the town hall. Before the day was over, eighty of the Medici's enemies had been killed.

In the confusion and swirling rumors, the crowd feared that Lorenzo had been killed or mortally wounded. To calm their fears, Lorenzo appeared on the balcony of the Medici Palace. He urged them to save their energy to defend the republic against the attacking army he felt sure would follow on the heels of the attempted coup. Through Lorenzo's efforts, at least one of the conspirators, the young Cardinal Raffaele Riario (son of Girolamo Riario), who had been celebrating the Mass at the moment of the attack, was protected from the crowd. Lorenzo had him brought to the Medici Palace and then sent him with an escort back to Rome.

The Pazzi family, however, was completely disgraced. Their names and coat-of-arms were ordered to be permanently erased by the Signoria. Their palace was confiscated and the name changed. Their family symbol — the dolphin — was cut down and destroyed wherever it was found. To this day, there is nothing in Florence marked with the sign of the dolphin.

Lorenzo had survived the assassination attempt. Giuliano had not. Florence was still firmly loyal to the Medici family. But Pope Sixtus was outraged at the indignities suffered by his family and the Archbishop of Pisa. He closed the Medici bank in Rome and seized its assets. He wanted to arrest the ambassador from Florence and all the Florentine bankers and merchants he could find. He was persuaded not to do so when reminded that his own great-nephew, Cardinal Riario, was still in Florence under Lorenzo's protection. But the Pope did issue a lengthy bull of excommunication against Lorenzo and those other citizens of Florence who were his accomplices. Finally, the Pope declared war on Florence and persuaded his closest ally, the King of Naples, to do the same.

The city of Florence stood firmly behind Lorenzo. They issued a defiant response to the Pope:

> "You say that Lorenzo is a tyrant and command us to expel him. But most Florentines call him their defender... Remember your high office as Vicar of Christ. Remember that the keys of St. Peter were not given to you to abuse in such a way... Florence will resolutely defend her liberties, trusting in Christ who knows the justice of her cause, and who does not desert those who believe in Him; trusting in her allies who regard her cause as their own; especially trusting in the most Christian King, Louis of France, who has ever been the patron and protector of the Florentine State."[8]

But the war did not go well for Florence. The forces of the Pope and the King of Naples outnumbered the forces of the Republic. King Louis of France, the traditional ally and protector of Florence, offered his sympathies, but declined to send troops. The Duchy of Milan, another traditional ally of Florence, was unable to send assistance either. The Duke of Milan had recently been assassinated in a family squabble and his widow and his brothers were arguing over who would control the city. The forces of the Republic met the invading army from the south at the borders, but were forced to slowly give ground because the invading army was larger.

After two years of warfare, with no prospect of victory in sight, Lorenzo took the bold step of going alone to visit one of the chief opponents of Florence — the King of Naples. He left an emotional letter to the Signoria explaining that since his enemies were the cause of the Republic's troubles, he hoped that his departure would deliver the Republic from its distress. The Signoria named Lorenzo as their Ambassador and, never expecting to see him again, wished him success on his mission to Naples. Lorenzo was 29 years old. Here is a portion of the letter that he left for the council:

> In the dangerous circumstances in which our city is placed, the time for deliberation is past. Action must be taken... I have decided with your approval to sail for Naples immediately, believing that as I am the person against whom the activities of our enemies are chiefly directed, I may, perhaps, by delivering myself into their hands, be the means of restoring peace to our fellow-citizens. As I have had more honor and responsibility among you than any private citizen has had in our day, I am more bound than any other person to serve our country, even at the risk of my life. With this intention I now go. Perhaps God wills that this war, which began in the blood of my brother and myself, should be ended by my means. My desire is that by my life or my death, my misfortune or my prosperity, I may contribute to the welfare of our city... I go full of hope, praying to God to give me grace to perform what every citizen should at all times be ready to perform for his country. I commend myself humbly to your Excellencies of the Signoria. Laurentius [Lorenzo] de' Medici.[9]

After 10 weeks of negotiation, Lorenzo succeeded in negotiating a costly peace with Naples. Lorenzo returned in triumph to Florence. In spite of the loss of territory and the tribute which must be paid to Naples, Lorenzo had ended the war and brought back peace to the Republic.

The Pope found himself facing the Republic of Florence alone. And then in the fall of 1480, a greater threat appeared which distracted all of Italy. A Turkish expeditionary force of 7,000 soldiers landed in southern Italy and immediately took control of the port of Otranto. Suddenly every city state in Italy saw the alarming prospect of a conquering Moslem army sweeping through the Italian peninsula. The Pope, the King of Naples, and the Northern Cities scurried to resolve their differences in order to face the external threat. Although the prospect of the invading Turkish army frightened almost everyone in Europe, the threat evaporated quickly.

In January of 1481, the Sultan died and the Turkish troops were recalled. But the peace which the Turkish threat had produced continued. As time went on the precarious truce among the Italian city-states persisted. The truce gradually lengthened into a period of real peace. For the last ten years of his life, Lorenzo's diplomatic efforts were all directed towards the goal of preserving peace among the Italian Cities.

He was helped in his efforts when, in 1484, the difficult, obstinate Pope Sixtus IV died. Lorenzo lost no time in ingratiating himself with his successor, Innocent VIII. Although Pope Innocent VIII had the usual list of relatives whom he worked to find positions for, he did not seek to dominate Italian politics, the way his predecessor had. For the rest of his life, Lorenzo once again enjoyed cordial relations with the Papacy, and once again the Rome branch of the Medici bank prospered.

With prosperity, maturity, and peace, Lorenzo was able to turn his attention to the things that truly interested him — painting, sculpture, poetry, and ancient literature.

Lorenzo became the patron and support of numerous artists and scholars: Pico della Mirandola (a gifted young philosopher), Filippino Lippi (son of the famous painter that Lorenzo's grandfather Cosimo had alternately supported and tried to reform), Ghirlandaio, Botticelli, Leonardo Da Vinci, and in later years, the young Michelangelo Buonarroti. In addition, Lorenzo became the chief patron and financial support of both the University

Adoration of the Magi *by Fra Filippino Lippi*

of Florence and the University of Pisa. With his support, Florence became widely known as the only university in Europe where the Greek language was adequately taught.

Lorenzo was interested enough in the arts that he founded a school for young artists in one of his houses in Florence. In his school, talented young artists not only learned the techniques of their craft, but were also taught about the literature and culture of the ancient Greek and Roman world. One of the first students at the Medici school was the young Michelangelo.

In the beginning of 1492, Lorenzo's health began to fail — though he was only 43. He spent his last months at the Medici country villa in Careggi. His strength declined rapidly and friends, writers, and artists all came to pay their respects. In April he died. His body was brought back to Florence and laid to rest in San Lorenzo, next to his brother Giuliano and not far from his grandfather and father. Pope Innocent VIII, on hearing of Lorenzo's death, exclaimed, "The peace of Italy is at an end."

Chapter 7

Girolamo Savonarola 1452-1498

When Lorenzo the Magnificent died in 1492, his 22 year old son, Piero succeeded him as head of the Medici family. Unfortunately, Piero lacked the strength of character and determination which had helped his father protect the Medici family interests in the turbulence of Italian politics. The adjectives which best described Piero di' Lorenzo de' Medici were spoiled and tactless. The tact and diplomacy of Lorenzo were sorely missed. And the enemies of the Medici were rallying behind a new leader — a fiery Dominican preacher and evangelist named Girolamo Savonarola.

Girolamo Savonarola was born at Ferrara in 1452. His father and grandfather had each served as court physician to the Duke of Ferrara. But life at the court held no appeal for Girolamo. At 22, he ran away from his family and joined the Dominican order as a monk. The Dominican order had been founded in order to teach and preach Christian doctrine and combat heresy. Any monk who showed skill as a public speaker was trained for the preaching ministry. Girolamo, after serving an apprenticeship at the monastery, was sent out to preach. In 1481, at the age 28, he came to Florence. Because of his preaching skills, he was appointed lector at the Dominican monastery of San Marco and invited to preach the Lenten sermons at the "Medici family church," San Lorenzo. In 1489 he settled permanently at the monastery of San Marco — that same monastery which had been rebuilt by Cosimo and was adorned with Fra Angelico's frescoes.

Gradually, Savonarola built up a following — more for his passion than his eloquence. In 1491 the large crowds for his Lenten sermons forced a move from the monastery to the largest church in town — the Cathedral or "Duomo." He preached a series of sermons on the coming judgement of God — which he claimed to know in some detail. He called upon the citizens to return to the simplicity of the early church and give up their wealth and riches. He told them that they must turn their back on Plato and Aristotle — who were both now rotting in hell; they must abandon luxuries and sensual pleasures; abolish gambling, horse racing, carnival, fine clothes. The rich should give their money to the poor. They must arrest prostitutes and burn sodomites.

In spite of his fiery sermons and the calls for repentance and denunciation of specific vices, Savonarola was tolerated by Lorenzo as long as he lived. As he lay dying at Careggio, Lorenzo sent word to Savonarola, asking him to visit. Lorenzo asked for, and received, his blessing before he died.

But, with Lorenzo gone, the passion of Savonarola's sermons increased. He continued to denounce the excesses of Florence, particularly its wealthy citizens, and especially Piero di' Lorenzo de' Medici.

"Repent, O Florence, while there is still time." Savonarola announced that he had seen a vision of a sword dangling over the city. He predicted that Florence would be judged and cleansed by invading barbarians pouring down from over the Alps.

In January of 1494, King Ferrante of Naples died. Charles VIII of France claimed the kingdom of Naples rightfully belonged to the king of France. Encouraged by Ludovico Sforza, Duke of Milan, he invaded Italy and started the long march towards Naples in Southern Italy with an army of 30,000 soldiers. Directly in the path of the invading French army lay the Republic of Florence. The "barbarians from over the Alps" reached the boundaries of the Republic in September. Charles demanded assistance from the Florentines and official recognition of his claim to be King of Naples.

Florence was in no position to oppose so large a force with her own small resources. No help could be expected from Milan — or Venice, Rome, or Naples for that matter.

Piero attempted to emulate his father and personally save the Republic by approaching Charles directly. He agreed immediately with all of Charles' demands — an enormous "loan" and the acceptance of French garrisons in all the key cities of the Republic. When he returned to Florence, the Signoria, far from welcoming him in triumph, slammed the door in his face and left Piero standing in the square outside the town hall. Before long an angry crowd gathered and a popular revolt against Medici rule broke out. The people believed that Charles and the invading French army were the fulfillment of the vision seen by Savonarola. They were sure that the barbarian army represented God's judgement on Florence and that it was pointless to resist them.

That night, Piero, his wife and his brother Giovanni, all fled the city. His remaining cousins in the city quickly changed their name from Medici to Popolano (which means "of the people") and removed the family crest from the walls of their house. A few days later, Charles VIII of France and his army entered Florence.

When the French army left the city the following week and continued their march southward towards Naples, Savonarola's followers took complete control of the city government. Savonarola proclaimed that God had called him to reform the city. He renewed his denunciations of wealth and finery, calling them "vanities." He called for a solemn procession and assembly in front of the town hall at which the "vanities" would be burned. Throughout Florence, families gathered their fine clothes, books, games, tapestries and artwork and brought them to the square. Botticelli and other artists brought their own canvases, denounced them as sensual and pagan, and laid them on the huge pile. Books, drawings, games, packs of cards, and other "vanities" were all brought forward and renounced by their owners. Then all was committed to the flames in a "Bonfire of the Vanities."

Meanwhile, the rest of Italy was organizing resistance to the invading French army. The Pope (Rodrigo Borgia) at length managed to unite the Italian cities into an alliance called The Holy League to oppose Charles. All of the Italian cities that is, except Florence. Savonarola continued to see Charles as God's instrument to judge Florence (and all of Italy) and so declined to join the League. Charles' line of supply was threatened however, and in the summer of 1495, he was forced to march his troops northward through Italy, over the Alps, and back to France.

With the French threat gone, the Pope summoned Savonarola to Rome to explain his actions. Savonarola declined the Pope's invitation and began to denounce the corruption at Rome in the same way he had attacked the "vanities" in Florence.

The Pope alternately threatened and attempted to bribe Savonarola. At one point he offered to appoint Savonarola a cardinal, if only he would give up preaching his fiery sermons. Savonarola only became more convinced of the Pope's corruption and worldliness. At one point, Savonarola concluded a reply to the Pope by asserting, "Your Holiness is well advised to make immediate provisions for your own salvation."

In June of 1497, the Pope excommunicated Savonarola. The people of Florence wavered in their support. Could the Pope be right and their Dominican monk wrong? Many in Florence had come to resent the attacks which Savonarola had launched on their favorite pastimes. In the midst of this turmoil, the leader of the Franciscans in Florence — long rivals to the Dominicans — challenged Savonarola to submit to a public test of the assertion that he enjoyed God's special favor. He challenged Savonarola to walk through fire to test God's favor — and offered to walk alongside him. Savonarola declined, but allowed one of his closest supporters to take up the challenge on his behalf.

The resort to a trial by ordeal further alienated many of the older families and councilmen who had either tolerated or supported Savonarola until now. When the day for the ordeal came, the two sides quarreled over the details for hours, until a sudden thunderstorm forced the cancellation of the ordeal for that day. The mood of the crowd turned ugly. The next day, Palm Sunday, 1498 there was a riot in the Duomo. The Dominican friar who was scheduled to preach was driven from the Cathedral amid a shower of rotten fruit and not a few stones. The crowd pursued the Dominicans to the monastery of San Marco. The monks locked the doors and defended themselves with pikes and stones hurled from the rooftop against the mob. Several townspeople were killed and the enraged crowd stormed into the monastery. A detachment of the town guard soon arrived with orders for Savonarola's arrest.

His support evaporated overnight. The city council of Florence tried Savonarola and two of his followers for promoting heresy and schism. They were found guilty and condemned to death. In April of 1498, Savonarola was burned at the stake in the town square and his ashes tossed into the river Arno.

Even with Savonarola dead, Piero di Lorenzo de' Medici never returned to Florence. A few years after the execution of Savonarola, Piero drowned crossing a river in southern Italy serving with the French army. His younger brother, Giovanni di Lorenzo de' Medici returned to Rome after a brief period in exile and reclaimed his position as a Cardinal and "prince of the church."

Chapter *8*

Sandro Botticelli 1445-1510

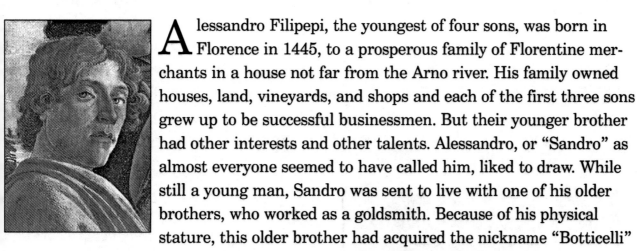 Alessandro Filipepi, the youngest of four sons, was born in Florence in 1445, to a prosperous family of Florentine merchants in a house not far from the Arno river. His family owned houses, land, vineyards, and shops and each of the first three sons grew up to be successful businessmen. But their younger brother had other interests and other talents. Alessandro, or "Sandro" as almost everyone seemed to have called him, liked to draw. While still a young man, Sandro was sent to live with one of his older brothers, who worked as a goldsmith. Because of his physical stature, this older brother had acquired the nickname "Botticelli" which means "little barrel." Although Sandro was tall and slender, he soon came to be known by his older brother's nickname as well and so "Alessandro Filipepi" became "Sandro Botticelli."

While working in his brother's shop, Sandro seems to have shown more ability (and certainly more interest) in drawing and design than in working as a goldsmith. Apparently his brother recognized his talent and resolved to help Sandro develop his talents to their fullest. And so, at the age of 19, Sandro entered the workshop of one of Florence's most famous painters, Fra Filippo Lippi, as an apprentice.

Sandro's apprenticeship with Fra Filippo was short, for four years later, his master died. But in that short time, Sandro had learned a great deal about drawing, sketching,

Fortitude *by Botticelli*

designing, and painting. His paintings were very much in the style of his master and they were very good. When Fra Filippo died in 1469, rather than joining another artist's workshop, Sandro established his own workshop and began accepting commissions from Florence's churches and leading citizens on his own.

One of his first commissions was for an allegorical painting called *Fortitude*, one of the seven virtues, commissioned by the civil court in Florence. The painting was an impressive success. The 25 year old Botticelli began to be spoken of as one of the great talents of Florence. In 1472, after three years on his own, he joined the painters guild as a master. At the same time he saw to it that his master's young son, Fra Filippino Lippi (15) was also registered.

Botticelli soon came to the attention of the Medici family and they began to regularly commission paintings from him and to recommend him to their friends. When Giuliano was killed and Lorenzo wounded in the assassination attempt of the Pazzi conspiracy, Botticelli was appalled. The city of Florence and the Medici family arranged for Botticelli to paint effigies of the conspirators on the wall of the Palazzo della Signoria (or town hall) where a number of them had been executed.

La Primavera *by Botticelli*

As a part of the general fascination with the study and revival of the ancient world sponsored by the Medici family, Botticelli was commissioned to paint several large canvases depicting scenes from Greek mythology. In 1477-1478 he painted perhaps his two most recognized works, *La Primavera* and *The Birth of Venus* — paid for by the great-nephews of Cosimo (first cousins of Lorenzo the Magnificent).

From 1480 to 1482 he worked in Rome (on loan from the Medici) on the frescos which adorned the walls of the Sistine chapel. The dispatch of Botticelli to Rome may have been a gesture of conciliation from Lorenzo to Pope Sixtus IV. There are still three enormous frescoes by Botticelli on the walls of the Sistine chapel — *Scenes from the Life of Moses,* the *Temptation of Christ*, and the *Destruction of the Children of Korah*.

He returned to Florence in 1482 — the same year Leonardo da Vinci departed for Milan. In 1482-1483 he painted several more classical scenes from Greek mythology: *Venus and Mars*, and *Pallas and the Centaur* (which has been described as an allegory showing how wisdom overcomes instinct).

In 1492 Lorenzo the Magnificent died. He had for many years been Botticelli's friend and patron (and was in fact, a few years younger than Sandro). In the next few years, Sandro seems to have become increasingly interested in the preaching and ideas of the new prior of the Dominican monastery in Florence, Girolamo Savonarola.

The Daughters of Jethro *by Botticelli*
The Sistine Chapel, Rome

After 1492, Botticelli's art begins to show dramatic changes in both style and content — perhaps the result of Botticelli's increasing interest and sympathy for Savonarola. Sandro had always painted works on religious themes and subjects — much of his income derived from works commissioned by churches or intended to decorate churches. But there is a new look to his religious paintings, a warmth and affection that had not been apparent earlier. And it seems that Sandro ceased work on paintings with mythological themes. Just from the titles of the pieces he painted, one gets a clear impression of where his interests now lay: *The Madonna of the Book, The Madonna of the Pomegranate, The Madonna of the Magnificat, The Bardi Madonna, The Annunciation, St. Augustine in his Study, The*

The Mystic Nativity *by Botticelli*

Communion of St. Jerome, Lamentation Over the Dead Christ, The Mystic Nativity, and *The Mystic Crucifixion*.

Sandro also developed an interest in the writings of Dante and did a series of engravings to illustrate an edition printed on one of the first printing presses in Florence.

When Savonarola called on the citizens of Florence to repent and give up their vanities, Sandro Botticelli was among those who responded. When Savonarola organized a "bonfire of the vanities" in the town square, Botticelli was among other Florentine artists who brought paintings and other works of art which they now deemed "vanities" and distractions from the Gospel. Botticelli tossed a number of his canvases onto the heap of valuables which were then consigned to the flames. If he ever later regretted the destruction of some of his own works, we have no record of it.

When Savonarola fell from favor and a Florentine Republic was established, Botticelli, now in his 40's, continued his work on religious paintings for wealthy patrons and churches. In 1504 (at the age of 59) he served on the committee appointed by the city of Florence to decide where to place Michelangelo's statue of *David*. The other committee members included Leonardo da Vinci and Filippino Lippi (the son of his original master). The Committee decided to place the statue in the town square in front of the city hall.

Botticelli's service on the *David* committee is almost his last recorded act as an artist. He was elderly and in poor health. He lived in retirement in Florence until his death in 1510 at the age of 65.

Chapter **9**

Leonardo da Vinci 1452-1519

Leonardo was the illegitimate son of a lawyer and a woman who may have been a servant in the house of Leonardo's grandparents. His father acknowledged his son and, though he later married, had no other children until after Leonardo was an adult. During his childhood, then, Leonardo was his father's only child. At an early age Leonardo began to display talents and abilities which marked him as a prodigy — a child of unusual intelligence and ability. One biographer tells the story of his study of arithmetic. Within a few months of starting his lessons, Leonardo was posing such difficult questions and had worked out so many theorems for himself that his instructor quit in doubt and confusion. Leonardo also had a love for music which became apparent while he was still young. He taught himself to play the lyre and often sang and accompanied himself. By all accounts his skill at music was impressive.

But above all, Leonardo loved to draw. He drew constantly and often worked in relief, carving figures in both wood and stone. Leonardo's father moved to Florence from his family's home in Vinci while Leonardo was quite young. Ser Paulo was soon a prominent lawyer and was elected to several posts in the city government. He seems for a while to have wanted Leonardo to follow in his footsteps and study law. But Leonardo's first love was always drawing. When he wasn't drawing he was visiting the workshops of various artists in Florence. Finally, when Leonardo was in his teens, his father took some of his drawings and showed them to one of his friends, the leading artist in Florence, Andrea del Verrochio. Andrea was amazed when he saw the drawings and urged Leonardo's

St John Baptizing Jesus
by Verrochio (and Leonardo da Vinci)

father to make arrangements for his son to study painting. Thus it was, that Leonardo came to begin his career as a painter in the workshop of Andrea del Verrochio in Florence.

As an apprentice in the workshop, Leonardo would have first been assigned the most menial of chores. Cleaning brushes, mixing paint, and preparing canvases for the artist and his more experienced assistants. But very soon after his arrival, Leonardo was already being given important responsibilities by the master, Verrochio. Verrochio assigned Leonardo to work on backgrounds and landscapes in some of the paintings he was working on. One day, the master asked his promising pupil to assist in drawing some of the smaller figures in an important painting he was completing for a local church.

The church had commissioned a painting showing *St. John baptizing Jesus* in the Jordan. In the lower left corner of the painting, Verrochio planned to show several angels holding Christ's robe. When the painting was finished, Verrochio stood inspecting it for a long time. It was clear that the figures of the angels were exquisite. They were so well drawn and painted that they drew one's eyes away from the central figures of John and Jesus which Verrochio had worked on. Verrochio sighed, broke his own paintbrush in two and turned to his young assistant, "From now on, you will do all the paintings in this workshop. The pupil has surpassed his master." From that time on, Verrochio devoted himself to sculpture and to the casting of bronze statues.

Greek and Roman artists had often worked in bronze, casting large statues of emperors and gods. During the Middle Ages, bronze statues ceased to be made. Only the bell-makers preserved the knowledge of how to work with molds and molten metal. In Florence, Ghiberti and Donatello revived the practice of casting bronze statues. Verrochio continued their work and became very skillful at working in bronze. In his workshop, Leonardo learned all that he could about the complicated process.

In 1476, Leonardo left Verrochio's workshop, aged 24, and began to work independently. That same year, Verrochio received a commission from the city of Venice to produce a bronze statue of one of its most famous military commanders, Bartolomeo Colleoni. The commission called for a statue of the general, seated on horseback, to be over 13 feet high. No bronze statue of this size had been attempted since the days of the Roman Empire. Leonardo immediately offered to return to Verrochio's workshop and help with the statue. Over the next few months, Leonardo made a detailed study of the anatomy of the horse. He filled hundreds of pages with sketches of horses in all sorts of poses, until he had mastered the horse. He knew how to draw a lifelike horse in any pose. He began to plan for the day when he would produce a large bronze statue of a figure mounted on horseback of his own.

In 1482, Leonardo got his wish. The Medici family in Florence had long been close friends with the Sforza family in Milan. The friendship went back to the days of Cosimo de' Medici and Francesco Sforza. The new ruler of Milan, Ludovico Sforza, had been begging Lorenzo de' Medici of Florence to send some Florentine artist of renown to Milan. Ludovico wished to have an impressive equestrian statue made, to honor his father, Francesco Sforza. The request of Ludovico Sforza and the desires of Leonardo were made known to Lorenzo, and Leonardo was dispatched to Florence's neighbor to the north, Milan.

When Leonardo entered the service of Ludovico Sforza, he was thirty years old. Milan was very different from Florence. The Sforza family ruled as absolute princes, the Dukes of Milan, rather than as simply leading citizens like the Medici. Ludovico's power rested on his well-trained army. His father, Francesco Sforza had been a mercenary soldier in the service of the Visconti family, the Dukes of Milan. Francesco Sforza won fame for his daring leadership in battle and married the daughter of the Duke of Milan. When the Duke died and the people rose in revolt against his heir, Francesco seized the opportunity and proclaimed himself the new Duke of Milan. His son, Ludovico had been given a humanist education and was a patron of the arts who delighted in music and theater. But Ludovico also acquired the military skills and ruthless political instincts of his father. Ludovico was immediately taken with Leonardo, both for his skill as an artist and his great wit and talent as a musician and stage designer.

The statue of Francesco Sforza that Ludovico and Leonardo planned was breath-taking. It would be over 30 feet high — twice the size of Verrochio's statue for Venice! No one had ever cast a bronze statue so large. Leonardo worked on sketches and designs for the statue and also on all the machinery and equipment that would be necessary for the production of the mold, casting the metal and moving the finished statue. But work progressed slowly. Leonardo was a perfectionist and often went back to revise details of every part of the plan.

While working on plans for the statue, Leonardo also found time to work on several paintings commissioned by the Sforza's. He also designed scenery and costumes for festivals and plays organized to entertain the family of the Duke of Milan. Work progressed on the statue very slowly. Eventually, more than ten years after starting, Leonardo had progressed as far as constructing a small model of the statue in wax. This model was universally praised for its lifelike and dramatic depiction of the horse rearing on two feet. Leonardo seems to have been much more fascinated with the figure of the horse than with the figure of Francesco Sforza. Privately he always referred to the statue as "the horse." Following his small model, Leonardo had a full-size model in clay constructed. This full-size model was then moved into the courtyard in the Sforza castle where it could be admired by the entire populace of Milan. Leonardo was finally making progress towards the actual casting of the statue when the French overthrew Ludovico and drove him out of Milan. Leonardo fled as well. The French troops saw the model statue of Francesco Sforza as one of the symbols of their defeated enemy, and so they destroyed it. Leonardo's towering bronze statue, twice the size of the one done by his master, Verrochio, was never completed.

The Last Supper *by Leonardo da Vinci*

While in Milan, Leonardo did complete a number of other works of art. One of the most famous is his painting of *The Last Supper*. In 1498, after waiting impatiently for years for work to proceed on "the horse," Ludovico Sforza commissioned Leonardo to paint Jesus and his Twelve Disciples at the Last Supper. The painting was to be done in the refectory (dining hall) of the Dominican monastery of Santa Maria della Grazie in Milan. Leonardo chose to portray the moment at which Jesus announces that one of the disciples will betray him. The expressions on the disciples' faces are remarkable. Some show love, some fear, some indignation, some sorrow. The painting itself was designed in such a way that it appeared to be an extension of the monk's dining hall. It appears that Jesus is offering the bread and wine to those seated not just in the painting, but also in the hall.

Leonardo, always a perfectionist, took a great deal of time in the planning and sketching of designs for The Last Supper. He often would spend hours staring at a portion of the drawing on the wall, making minor corrections and refinements. The prior of the monastery was impatient with Leonardo's slow progress. Eventually he complained to the Duke of Milan that Leonardo was lazy, often spending half the day simply staring into space. The Duke of Milan listened patiently to the prior and then sent for Leonardo. He asked Leonardo, very patiently, to explain to the prior the reasons for his slow, painstaking way of working. Leonardo slowly explained to the Duke (he refused to even address his remarks to the prior) that often, the greatest artists accomplish more when they actually do very little. For while they are lost in contemplation, they are perfecting their ideas, so that when they turn to actually creating with their hands, their ideas have been perfected and need little or no revision. Then, Leonardo added to the Duke that he still had to complete the sketches and design for two of the heads in the painting — the head of Christ, for which he was unwilling to seek a model on earth and the head of Judas. For Judas, he said he found it difficult to imagine the face of a man who was so wicked that he could have resolved to betray his Lord and the Creator of the World. "None the less," continued Leonardo, "I will search for a model for Judas, but if I am unable to find anything, there is always the head of the prior, who is so insistent and indiscreet!" This caused the Duke of Milan to laugh out loud, and the poor confused prior returned to the monastery and left Leonardo in peace.

After the French troops overthrew Ludovico Sforza, Leonardo returned to his home in Florence. He had been gone for seventeen years, but his reputation as a great artist had been by no means diminished. He began receiving commissions from the leading citizens and churches of the city almost as soon as he returned.

In 1502 he worked for some months as a military engineer for the legendary prince, Cesare Borgia. When the Duke of Romagna's shooting star had fallen to earth, he quietly returned to his workshop in Florence. Sometime after his return to Florence, he was commissioned by a wealthy merchant to paint a portrait of his wife. All of Leonardo's remarkable skill as a painter is on display in this painting, technically titled La Gioconda, but known throughout the world as the *Mona Lisa*. Leonardo worked on the portrait for four years and it is universally acknowledged to be a work of artistic perfection.

La Gioconda (*Mona Lisa*) by *Leonardo da Vinci*

In 1503, the city of Florence completed an addition to the city hall — a new council chamber, which could seat 500. To decorate the walls of this new chamber, the city commissioned its two most famous artists (and fierce rivals), Leonardo and Michelangelo, to each complete a scene depicting an important battle in the history of the Florentine Republic. Leonardo, who had always disliked Michelangelo and felt more than a little rivalry with him, made elaborate and impressive plans for his battle scene.

> "It would be impossible to express the inventiveness of Leonardo's design for the soldier's uniforms, which he sketched in all their variety, or the crests of the helmets and other ornaments, not to mention the incredible skill he demonstrated in the shapes and feature of the horses, which Leonardo, better than any other master, created with their boldness, muscles, and graceful beauty."
> — **Giorgio Vasari,** ***The Lives of the Artists***[10]

In order to achieve the effect he wanted, Leonardo studied ancient texts which described various ways of painting murals on vertical surfaces. Leonardo wanted to achieve a stunning triumph that would outshine his rival. He found an ancient text that gave instructions for how to achieve a high-gloss, bright, vibrant finish by mixing wax with the pigments before they were applied to the walls. Unfortunately, Leonardo misunderstood the instructions in the ancient texts and the proportions of wax and pigment that he used were incorrect. When he had finished the painting and began the final step of curing the paint by heating the room with large braziers, the wax and pigments melted, merged, and ran down the wall into a puddle on the floor. Several years of work were destroyed in a few minutes. Michelangelo's painting was never finished either — never progressing beyond initial designs and sketches.

The last ten years of his life, Leonardo spent in Milan and Rome where he was offered several important commissions by Pope Leo X (Giovanni de' Medici). In 1517, King Francis I of France invited Leonardo to move to France where the king would provide him with a house, servants, and a stipend and no specific requirement or commissions. Leonardo was pleased by the opportunity to pursue his own interests and research and took the French King up on his offer. Francis bestowed upon Leonardo the title of "first painter, architect, and mechanic of the King." Leonardo worked on a variety of projects and filled many notebooks with his studies of flight, mechanics, hydraulics, and anatomy. Towards the end of his life he began to regret that so many of his projects, like "the horse" of Milan remained unfinished. Many his notebook pages contained the repeated line, "Tell me if anything at all was done, tell me if anything at all was done..."

In 1519, Leonardo's health took a turn for the worse. The King of France hurried to join him at his bedside. On May 2nd, he died quietly in bed at the age of seventy-five.

Chapter 10

Michelangelo Buonarroti
1475-1564

Michelangelo was born in 1475 to an aristocratic (if somewhat impoverished) family in Florence. He showed some academic ability as a youth and his parents enrolled him in schools which might have led to a career as a notary or a lawyer. But all Michelangelo wanted to do was draw. He spent all the time he could drawing in secret. His father was not pleased, considering artists to be little more than trained craftsmen, like carpenters or masons. But Michelangelo persisted, in spite of his parents' objections. Finally, his father relented, and in 1488 he apprenticed the 14-year old Michelangelo to the leading artist in Florence, Domenico Ghirlandaio.

Michelangelo's skill and character grew rapidly and Ghirlandaio soon considered him his star pupil. One year after Michelangelo had been apprenticed, Lorenzo de' Medici decided that he wished to do something to revive the ancient art of sculpture. Florence had produced many great painters, but there were still no sculptors whose works could compare with the works of the Greeks and Romans. Lorenzo began a school in the garden of the Medici palace, employing as instructor, Bertoldo, a sculptor who had learned his craft from Donatello. Lorenzo asked Ghirlandaio to send him two of his best students, giving special attention to any who seemed to have a gift for sculpture. One of the two whom Ghirlandaio sent was the 15 year old Michelangelo.

For four years, Michelangelo studied sculpture in the garden of the Medici palace. He quickly became a favorite of Lorenzo. Lorenzo invited Michelangelo to live in the Medici palace and treated him like a son. He took his meals at the Medici table, seated along with Lorenzo's children.

After Lorenzo's death, Michelangelo returned home and lived with his own parents, but he continued his work in sculpture and painting. He remained a great favorite with Piero, the son of Lorenzo the Magnificent. Michelangelo received many commissions for works of art from the Medici and from other wealthy Florentine families, as well as from the area's many churches and monasteries.

In 1494, just before the French invasion and the overthrow of Piero, Michelangelo left Florence for Bologna. After a year's absence, he returned to Florence and resumed his work there.

In 1495, Michelangelo finished a sculpture of a sleeping cupid. One of his friends admired the work immensely. He said it was as good or better than anything done by the ancient Roman sculptors. In fact, he suggested, if Michelangelo were to stain the marble and bury it so that it appeared to be an Ancient Roman sculpture, he could sell it in Rome for far more money than if it were presented in Florence as something new. Michelangelo did as his friend suggested and sold the cupid through an intermediary to a Cardinal in Rome for a large sum of money. But, somehow, the Cardinal heard the truth of the matter from friends in Florence. Though he demanded his money back, he sent for Michelangelo to come to Rome and take up residence at the Cardinal's palace.

The Pieta *by Michelangelo*

While staying in Rome, Michelangelo received commissions from many of the "princes of the church" and wealthy Roman families. His skill as a sculptor increased with each passing month. One of his most famous pieces of sculpture, The Pieta, was completed during this period. In The Pieta, Mary holds the body of Christ in her lap and mourns the death of her son. It is still admired as one of the most perfect pieces of sculpture ever created. The completion of The Pieta brought Michelangelo a great deal of fame as a sculptor.

David *by Michelangelo*

In 1501, after the fall of Savonarola, Michelangelo's friends (and Soderini, the new Chancellor of the Republic) persuaded him to return to Florence. The leaders of the Republic were eager to commission an impressive sculpture from Michelangelo. There was a large block of marble, over sixteen feet high, which had stood in the workshop of the Cathedral for many years. Several artists had considered using it for a colossal sculpture, but none had ventured so far as to start carving. Leonardo da Vinci had even expressed interest in working with the large block. Based on the reputation he had acquired in Rome, Michelangelo was given the block of marble and told to create a statue worthy of the newly independent Florentine Republic.

For two years, he worked on his carving of *David*, the shepherd boy. Michelangelo depicted him at the moment just before he launches his attack on Goliath, stern and purposeful. David holds his sling and stone and contemplates the Philistine who mocks the armies of the living God. When the statue was completed in 1504, it was immediately recognized as a masterpiece. The Council of Florence placed it in the square in front of the town hall. There it stood for many years as a symbol of the spirit of the Florentine Republic and the triumphant, optimistic, spirit of the Renaissance.

In 1506, Michelangelo returned to Rome, where he was commissioned to work on the tomb of Pope Julius II. Pope Julius wished his tomb to be larger and more imposing than any other in Rome. Michelangelo drew a plan that included a huge sarcophagus, surrounded on all four sides by life-size pieces of sculpture. After he completed his plans, Michelangelo spent 8 months supervising the cutting of marble blocks in the quarry at Carrara. But when he returned to Rome, Pope Julius refused to see him, or authorize any further work on the tomb. Michelangelo was furious and angrily left Rome and returned to Florence. He was 32. For almost a year he ignored repeated requests from the Pope to return to Rome.

When he did return, Julius still refused to let Michelangelo continue on the tomb. Instead, he asked Michelangelo to design and execute a series of frescoes to decorate the ceiling of the Sistine Chapel. The space for the frescoes was huge, almost 6,000 square feet. Michelangelo divided the ceiling into nine panels — six tell the story of Creation and The

The Creation of Adam *by Michelangelo*

Fall, three are scenes from the story of Noah and the Flood. The most famous portion is the fourth panel which shows *The Creation of Adam*. God leans down from the clouds and touches his finger to the outstretched figure of the reclining Adam.

Pope Julius died in 1513 and was succeeded by Giovanni de'Medici, who took the name Leo X. Michelangelo was no stranger to the new Pope. They had shared meals together when Michelangelo was growing up in the Medici palace in Florence. Leo commissioned additional works of art from his old friend, Michelangelo.

After Leo's death, his successors continued their patronage of Michelangelo. In 1534,

The Last Judgement *by Michelangelo, The Sistine Chapel*

the newly elected Pope Paul III asked Michelangelo to paint *The Last Judgement*, on the front wall of the Sistine Chapel. The size of this scene, like the frescoes on the ceiling which Michelangelo had completed earlier for Pope Julius, is immense. It contains over 300 figures. Michelangelo worked on it for seven years, finishing it in 1541. He was 66 years old.

After he finished *The Last Judgement*, he resumed work on the tomb of Julius II. The original plans had been greatly reduced, but the Pope's family still wished to see his tomb completed. Michelangelo finished this work in 1545.

That same year, in 1545, Pope Paul III appointed Michelangelo chief architect of the Vatican. His duties included supervising the completion of the church of St. Peter in Rome. Michelangelo reviewed and revised the

plans of earlier architects and spent a great
deal of energy in supervising the workmen.
He visited the work site almost every day to
review their progress.

From 1545-1550 he also worked on two
frescoes for Pope Paul III, *The Conversion of
St. Paul* and *The Martyrdom of St. Peter*.
The work was hard on him though. He commented to a friend that "Painting in fresco
is not for old men." Michelangelo was 75
years old when they were finished.

St. Peter's in Rome

The last years of his life were spent working on one final sculpture, called *The Deposition*. This sculpture depicts the body of
Jesus as it is being removed from the cross,
supported by Mary Magdalene and Mary the
mother of Jesus. Standing behind the group is
Joseph of Arimathea. His face expresses his
great sorrow. The face of Joseph is, in fact,
Michelangelo's own self-portrait, an indication
that he intended the group to be his own
grave monument. The sculpture is now in the
Duomo in Florence beneath Brunelleschi's
dome. Though he worked on the sculpture off
and on for many years, it was still unfinished
when he died.

For the rest of his life, Michelangelo
spent most of his time supervising the work
on St. Peter's Cathedral. Every day he rode
on horseback through the narrow streets of
Rome to check on the progress of the stone-
cutters and carpenters. Leonardo had died
thirty years before, in 1519 at the court of
the French king. Raphael had died in 1520,

The Deposition *by Michelangelo*

at the premature age of 37. For more than 30 years, Michelangelo had been the most celebrated living artist in all of Italy.

Inspired by the Duomo in Florence, he set out self-consciously to design its sister for St. Peters in Rome. In January of 1564, he was still working daily in his workshop with hammer and chisel. But in the chilly Roman winter, he caught cold and weakened steadily. He died in February, a few weeks before his 90th birthday.

His coffin lay in state in Rome for several days and thousands of Romans came to pay their respects. As he wished then, his body was taken back to Florence (secretly, since the people of Rome wanted Michelangelo buried in their city as well). In Florence, Michelangelo's coffin was mobbed. Men fought for the honor of carrying it. After a state funeral, attended by hundreds, he was buried in the Medici church of San Lorenzo.

The Ceiling of the Sistine Chapel by Michelangelo

Chapter 11

Cesare Borgia 1475-1507

C ardinal Rodrigo Borgia, was a short, somewhat overweight and ugly Spaniard. He was also, by all accounts, quite charming. Women in particular were fascinated by him. Cardinal Borgia, like many high officials of the Roman Catholic Church in the late 1400's, was neither celibate nor humble. He was greedy and ambitious, as well as clever and charming. It was a dangerous mix of qualities. Rodrigo had come to Rome from his native Spain in 1449 when he had been appointed a Cardinal by his uncle, Pope Calixtus III (Alfonso Borgia). By 1475, Cardinal Borgia had accumulated a great fortune through the numerous church offices which he held — among the most important of which was the office of vice-chancellor of the Church, 2nd in command only to the Pope himself.

In 1475, Rodrigo's mistress gave birth to a son, his second child. Rodrigo named the child Cesare, the Italian variant of the name Caesar (see Famous Men of Rome for more information about Julius Caesar, Cesare's namesake).

Rodrigo gave his sons an education fit for a prince. Cesare's first tutors taught him Latin and Greek and introduced him to the writings of Cicero, Julius Caesar, Tacitus, Livy, Herodotus, and Thucydides. He learned the history and the politics of Greece and Rome at an early age. He was also trained as a prince in the martial arts. He learned to ride, to fight, and to hunt. In 1489, at the age of 14, he left Rome and enrolled in the

University of Perugia. There he studied law. Two years later, he transferred to the University of Pisa where one of his fellow students was Giovanni de' Medici, the son of Lorenzo the Magnificent. Cesare was not only the wealthiest student at the university, but he also demonstrated that he was one of the most gifted as well. He excelled in his studies and demonstrated his eloquence in public debate on matters of the law.

In 1492, after the death of Pope Innocent VIII, Rodrigo Borgia was elected Pope by the College of Cardinals and took the name Pope Alexander VI. His illegitimate son Cesare, 17 years old, left the University of Pisa, and returned to Rome to join his father. He was gifted and arrogant and about to embark on a short, meteoric career that was both stunning and horrifying.

Cesare's father was much more concerned with worldly power than with serving honorably as the Vicar of Christ. Within a month of his election as pope, Cesare's father appointed him archbishop of Valencia. Cesare's elder brother Juan, was appointed captain-general of the Church, commander-in-chief of all of the papacy's armed forces. (Yes, the Pope had his own army!) Their younger sister, Lucrezia, was betrothed to a young nobleman of the Sforza family — the ruling family of Milan — as a part of Pope Alexander's grand plan to establish the Borgia family as a permanent, powerful player in Italian politics. In 1493, Pope Alexander (Cesare's father) set about making Cesare a Cardinal.

In the summer of 1494 came the cataclysmic invasion of Italy by a French army under the command of King Charles VIII. Charles VIII claimed the title of King of Naples and he insisted that the city-states of Italy grant his army free passage through their territory so that he could assert his claims in Naples.

> "Although I am a Spaniard, not the less for that do I love Italy, nor do I wish to see Italy in the hands of anyone but Italians."
>
> — **Pope Alexander** *to the Duke of Ferrara during the invasion by the French Army.*[11]

As King Charles VIII approached Rome (for the effect of his army's advance on Florence see the chapter on Savonarola), Alexander gave orders to open the gates of the city of Rome to the French army. Meanwhile Pope Alexander and his son Cesare fled to the fortress of the Castel Sant'Angelo. But after a siege of only a few days, they negotiated a surrender with Charles. The Pope's terms were very shrewd. He was forced to surrender Cesare as a prisoner and hostage and to grant the French army free passage through the Papal States. But he managed to get King Charles to recognize the Pope's political authority over his territory in Italy and his spiritual authority over the entire church (including the church in France). King Charles further agreed to obey the Pope in all spiritual matters and to act as his protector against political rivals in Italy.

Shortly after Charles departure from Rome on his way towards Naples, Cesare managed to escape from the French army and made his way to Northern Italy where he began to forge an anti-French alliance between the papacy, Venice, and Milan. Florence under Savonarola declined to join — a fact that infuriated Cesare and Pope Alexander. Spain and the Holy Roman Empire were persuaded to support the alliance against the French as well.

King Charles, too late, realized his precarious position. With a hostile alliance now in place in Northern Italy, his communication, supply route, and line of retreat back to French territory was in serious danger. He turned his army north, resolved to fight his way back to France if necessary. The Italian armies intercepted the French near Fornovo in Northern Italy on July 5th, 1495 and engaged them in a bloody battle. Neither side emerged as the clear victor, though the French did lose their baggage train and most of the riches they had looted from Florence, Rome, & Naples. But they were able to withdraw and continue their retreat, safely reaching France soon after.

Cesare had learned a great deal from the events of the French invasion. He took the measure of the rulers of the Italian cities and long remembered how they had reacted to the threat of French troops. The knowledge of who had been courageous and who had been cowardly he used to his own advantage.

In January of 1497, Pope Alexander launched a military campaign against one of the prominent families in the papal states — the Orsini. The papal forces were nominally under the command of Pope Alexander's oldest son (and Cesare's elder brother), Juan Borgia. The papal forces managed to defeat the Orsini, but Juan proved to be an incompetent bungler. The victory came because of the skill of his allies and lieutenants, though Juan claimed the credit for it. There were rumors that Juan was a coward who had fled the field at the start of one battle.

In June of 1497, Cesare was appointed papal legate by his father in order to attend the coronation of King Federigo of Naples. At the same time, Alexander granted his son, Juan, the hereditary title of Duke of Terracina and Pontecorvo, two cities which were a part of the Papal states. Enemies of the Borgia family were outraged. The Pope was plainly taking steps to establish the Borgia's as the hereditary rulers of central Italy, regardless of who should be named the next Pope.

On June 16, 1497, Juan Borgia's body was found drowned in the Tiber River. His father, Pope Alexander, seems to have been grief-stricken by the death of his eldest son. There is no proof that Cesare Borgia was involved in the death of his elder brother, but many in Rome were certain that he had been. After Juan's death, Cesare became the heir to all of the Borgia fortunes. As a cardinal, he might have been expected to be a contender to be named Pope after the death of his father. Father and son seem to have developed other plans, however. Pope Alexander wanted to establish the Borgia family as the hereditary rulers of the territory in central Italy known as the Papal States, with a hereditary title — perhaps the "Duke of Rome" — which could be kept in the family and passed from father to son. The problem with the Papacy was that the office could not be automatically passed to one's offspring.

Since Cesare was a Cardinal, he could not legitimately become the founder of dynastic line. Pope Alexander and Cesare decided therefore, that Cesare should renounce his position as Cardinal and resume life as a layman, released from his vows of chastity and service to the church.

Pope Alexander summoned an extraordinary meeting of the college of Cardinals. Though scandalized by the Pope's plans, and suspicious that Cesare was in fact, the murderer of his own brother, the Cardinals were forced to grant Alexander's request. The Pope, as reported by the Venetian ambassador, "was given license that the Cardinal of Valencia, son of the Pope, could put off the hat and make himself a soldier and get himself a wife."

The Pope now reversed himself and began to forge an alliance with the French in opposition to both Milan and Naples. He hoped to use his alliance with the French to secure the position of the Borgia family as preeminent in Italy. He sent Cesare to France in hopes of arranging his marriage to a French princess and thus cement an alliance between the Borgia's and the French. In May of 1499, Cesare was married to Charlotte d'Albret, daughter of a prominent French nobleman, the Duke of Valentinois. Although the marriage was arranged for purely strategic reasons, the ironic fact is that Cesare seems to have actually liked Charlotte, and she returned his favor.

October 6, 1499 Louis XII of France marched his army into Milan (accompanied by Cesare Borgia). From there, Cesare departed in command of a contingent of French troops to effect the conquest of the Romagna and so to establish Borgia rule in Italy. He quickly took the cities of Forli and Cesena. But before he could proceed with the conquest of Pesaro, Rimini, and Faenza, his French troops were recalled to Milan.

On February 26th, Cesare made a triumphal entry into Rome. At the age of 24, he thought of himself as a prince, the heir to a great family dynasty, and perhaps as the reincarnation of Julius Caesar. In July, Cesare ordered the assassination of his brother-in-law, Alfonso, Duke of Bisceglie, Lucrezia's husband — because of his support of Naples and opposition to the Borgia alliance with the French.

On October 1st, 1500 Cesare set out with an army of 10,000 French soldiers to finish the conquest of the Romagna. Pesaro and Rimini surrendered and pronounced their allegiance to Cesare before his armies arrived. The rest of the province proved easy to subdue by Cesare's forces.

On May 15th, 1501 in a ceremony in Rome, Pope Alexander formally invested Cesare as Duke of Romagna. In December, Pope Alexander and Cesare succeeded in arranging the wedding of Lucrezia with Alfonso d'Este, heir to the Duchy of Ferrara, a small but strategically important city-state situated between Venice and the Romagna.

For the next six months, Pope Alexander and Cesare were quiet. But the cardinals and nobles of Italy were certain that they were plotting something.

In June of 1502, events began to unfold suddenly. The citizens of the Florentine city of Arezzo rebelled. On the same day, the city of Pisa seceded from Florence and offered Cesare lordship of their city. Simultaneously, Cesare joined an army of 6,000 infantry and 700 horsemen at Spoleto and began to march towards Urbino. Faced with the sudden distraction of his major ally, Florence, and Borgia troops closing in from three directions, the Duke of Urbino fled, leaving the Duchy to be snapped up by Cesare. It was an astonishing coup which took the breath of the other Italian nobles. Cesare, barely 27 years old, was clearly a formidable opponent.

In the summer of 1502, Cesare hired Leonardo da Vinci to assist him in a number of projects. Leonardo laid out new building plans for several of Cesare's cities. More importantly, he prepared a series of detailed maps of the territory of the Papal states that would be an invaluable aid to Cesare and his military commanders in any future campaigns.

In October of 1502 news reached Alexander that just about every Italian petty lord hostile to the Borgias had attended a meeting convened by Cardinal Orsini. The conspirators included many of those who had served as military lieutenants in Cesare's campaigns. It seemed clear that a conspiracy was being hatched and that its target was the Borgia's, probably Cesare's cities in the Romagna. Cesare appeared unperturbed, but he took immediate steps to assemble as large a force of armed men as possible. While the conspirators vacillated, Cesare's forces grew stronger and stronger. When his numbers swelled to overwhelming, the conspirators began to get cold feet and opened negotiations with Cesare. Cesare appeared willing to strike bargains with each of them separately. Then, in December, Cesare suddenly marched his troops to the town of Senigallia, where five of his former commanders were staying. He quickly took them prisoner, executed two, and imprisoned the other three. Cesare's ruthlessness shocked and impressed all of Italy. He now seemed more secure than ever in his title of Duke of Romagna.

But at the height of their power, in the summer of 1503, both Pope Alexander and his son Cesare were struck down with malaria. On August 18th, Pope Alexander died. All of Cesare's enemies seized the opportunity to rise against him. The city of Venice supported the former rulers of the cities of the Romagna as they sought to return and reclaim the cities they had ruled before being expelled by Cesare. A few of Cesare's lieutenants remained loyal and several cities held fast in their loyalty to him.

Meanwhile, Cesare was working furiously behind the scenes to influence the election of the new Pope. He desperately needed to insure that his own position would not be attacked. On September 22nd, Francesco Piccolomini was elected Pope and took the name Pius III. Barely two weeks later, the new Pope re-appointed Cesare to his position as Captain-General of all the Papal forces. Cesare began to make plans for a military campaign to recapture the cities of the Romagna. But it was not to be. Pius III was 63 and in poor health. On October 17th, after reigning as Pope for less than a month, Pius III died, another victim of the malaria outbreak which had claimed Pope Alexander. Cesare's position was once again precarious. Ten days later, Cesare struck a deal with one of the most powerful Cardinals, Guilio della Rovere. In return for Cesare's support in the papal election (Cesare still controlled the votes of a significant faction in the college of Cardinals), della Rovere promised to reappoint Cesare as Captain-General of the Papal forces and to support his reconquest of the Romagna.

Guilio della Rovere took the name, Pope Julius II. But once elected Pope, della Rovere declined to carry out his half of the bargain and Cesare found himself betrayed. By December, Cesare was a prisoner, under house arrest, in his own apartments in the Vatican. Cesare conceded defeat to Julius and began to negotiate the terms of his release. He was forced to surrender all claims and strongholds in the territory of the Romagna. The Duke of Romagna had lost all of his possessions. Once freed, Cesare fled Rome to Naples. But Cesare had many enemies, and 8 months after he arrived in Naples, he was arrested, placed on board ship, transported to Spain and delivered into the custody of King Ferdinand and Queen Isabella.

After spending two years as a prisoner in various Spanish castles, Cesare managed to arrange his escape. He fled to the tiny kingdom of Navarre, on the border between France and Spain. Navarre was ruled by King Jean d'Albret, the brother of his French wife (whom he had not seen since his departure from France in October of 1499). Cesare was welcomed by his brother-in-law (who seems to have aided in the planning of his escape) who offered him a position as a military commander in the army of the Kingdom of Navarre.

In 1507, while conducting a campaign against a rebellious nobleman of Navarre, Cesare charged foolishly into an ambush, was unhorsed and mortally wounded by a terrible lance thrust. His brother-in-law had him buried in the church of Santa Maria in the town of Viana in the kingdom of Navarre. The inscription on his marble tomb reads "Here lies he whom all the world feared." The man whom Machiavelli used as his model for The Prince was dead at the age of 32.

Chapter 12

Niccolo Machiavelli 1469-1527

Niccolo Machiavelli was born in 1469, the year a young Lorenzo the Magnificent assumed his position as head of the Medici family and first citizen of Florence. He died in 1527, the year that the German troops of Emperor Charles V sacked Rome. His life spans the final years of the Italian Renaissance and saw the opening events of the Reformation. He was born into a distinguished Florentine family with a long history of political office. His parents provided an education for him that was designed for a career as a public official — as a notary and lawyer.

When Niccolo was 25, in 1494, French troops marched through Florence, and the Medici were overthrown and fled into exile. Four years later, after the execution of Savonarola, the Florentine Republic was established under the leadership of Soderini. Niccolo was appointed Second Chancellor of the Republic. He was also appointed secretary to the Defense Committee. The Defense Committee had much to do. Florence faced successive threats from the French in 1499 (under Louis XII), from Cesare Borgia, and then from the forces of Pope Julius II.

The Chancellor of the Florentine Republic, Soderini, was a learned Italian humanist with a passion for Greek.. He left much of the day-to-day work in the hands of Niccolo. Niccolo was sent on frequent diplomatic missions abroad, representing Florence in negotiations with other Italian cities, as well as France and Germany.

During Cesare's coup against Urbino in June of 1502, Niccolo was sent by the city of Florence to negotiate an armistice. The younger Cesare's self-confidence and command of the situation made a deep impression on Niccolo.

Niccolo was fascinated by the way in which Cesare dealt with the rebellion of his former lieutenants. He wrote a detailed account of Cesare's calm mastery of the situation, his cunning in luring his former lieutenants to a peace conference and his swift justice once he had the rebels in his power. For Niccolo, this was an example of successful statecraft.

As Niccolo continued in service to the Republic of Florence, he was promoted from Secretary of the Defense Committee to Minister of Defense. One of his most important projects was the organization of a militia drawn from inside the Florentine Republic. In the past, Florence had depended on mercenaries (hired soldiers) to fight its battles. In the struggle to recover Pisa (which had rebelled at the instigation of Cesare Borgia), Niccolo employed his militia with great skill and won an impressive series of victories.

In 1512, the forces of Pope Julius II defeated Florence and placed the Medici family back in power. Niccolo had held office in the Republic for so long that the Medici did not trust him. Niccolo found himself without political employment and retired (at the age of 43) to a little villa just outside the city of Florence. In spite of his 14 years of service and high political office he does not seem to have amassed a fortune. What little wealth he had seems to have come from his inheritance from his father.

No longer a politician, Niccolo spent his time writing about politics. Over the years, he produced a remarkable series of works: *The History of Florence, On the Art of War,* and *Discourses on the First Ten Books of Livy.*

But of course, the book he is most remembered for is titled *The Prince.* Written in 1513, just after the defeat of the Republic and the restoration of the Medici, it is still not clear to modern scholars exactly why Machiavelli wrote the book.

The ideas in the book were shocking when Machiavelli wrote them, and they are still shocking today.

> "*The Prince* lays down as a major premise that men in general are selfish, treacherous, cowardly, greedy, and, above all, gullible and stupid. It there-fore advises a prince, and particularly a new prince who hopes to destroy the liberties of those he rules, to employ hypocrisy, cruelty, and deceit, to make

himself feared even at the risk of making himself hated, to divide the people and destroy their natural leaders, and to keep faith with no one, since no one will keep faith with him. It views the world of politics as a jungle in which moral laws and standards of ethical conduct are merely snares for fools, a jungle in which there is no reality but power, and power is the reward of ruthlessness, ferocity and cunning. In such a jungle, not the actual Cesare Borgia, but the picture of himself which Cesare succeeded in conveying at the height of his fame, a savage beast — half lion and half fox — would be the natural king."

— **Garrett Mattingly**[12]

Why Machiavelli would write such a book and address it to the new Medici princes who ruled in Florence — where he had held high office in the Republic — is a mystery. The book was denounced almost as soon as it was written. The Catholic church placed it on the index of books which Christians were forbidden to read. After the start of the Reformation, Protestants accused Catholics of using it as their guide to statecraft. Henry VIII's chancellor, Thomas Cromwell is supposed to have owned and studied a copy of the book. The statements in the book are so outrageous, that some have concluded that it is not intended seriously, but that it is a satire — that Machiavelli intended it as a warning about how princes are likely to behave.

Some have taken the position that Machiavelli is simply a historian writing about the things he had observed and read about in history and describing what he finds to have worked, without making any moral judgments. But Machiavelli himself does not pretend to be neutral in *The Prince*. In *The Prince*, Machiavelli praises those tactics which succeed. He is very critical of the traditional virtues of honesty and loyalty, since, he believes, these would often prevent a prince from acquiring or maintaining his power. Machiavelli was not interested in theories, he wanted to know what worked. In a letter to a friend he wrote, "What interests me more than theory is what is, what has been, and what may reasonably happen."

Whatever Machiavelli intended in his writings, men down through the ages have used it as a guide for political action. What Machiavelli himself intended remains something of a mystery.

Machiavelli spent the remaining years of his life in retirement on his country estate. When he died in 1527, he was still working on an unfinished, multivolume history of the city of Florence.

The Medici Family

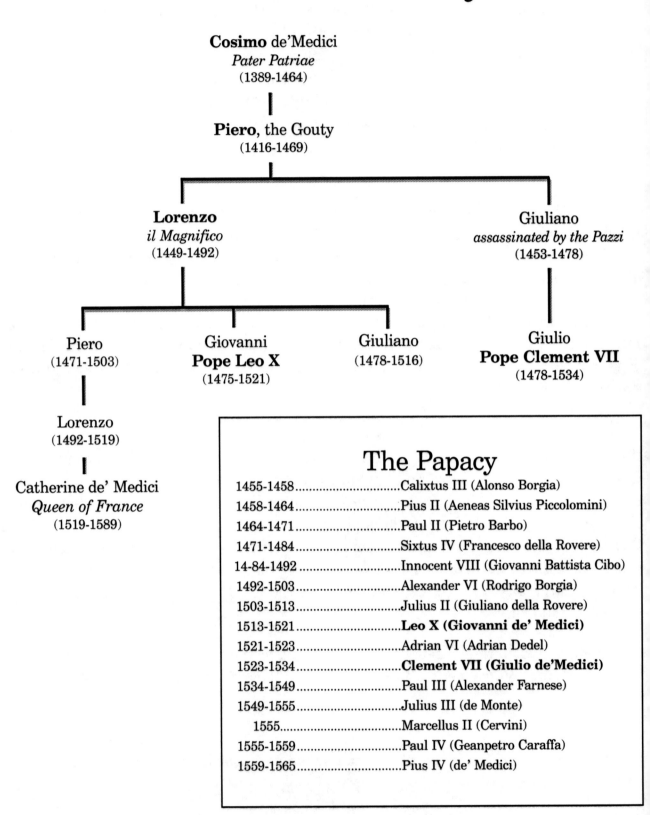

Cosimo de'Medici
Pater Patriae
(1389-1464)

Piero, the Gouty
(1416-1469)

Lorenzo
il Magnifico
(1449-1492)

Giuliano
assassinated by the Pazzi
(1453-1478)

Piero
(1471-1503)

Giovanni
Pope Leo X
(1475-1521)

Giuliano
(1478-1516)

Giulio
Pope Clement VII
(1478-1534)

Lorenzo
(1492-1519)

Catherine de' Medici
Queen of France
(1519-1589)

The Papacy

1455-1458	Calixtus III (Alonso Borgia)
1458-1464	Pius II (Aeneas Silvius Piccolomini)
1464-1471	Paul II (Pietro Barbo)
1471-1484	Sixtus IV (Francesco della Rovere)
14-84-1492	Innocent VIII (Giovanni Battista Cibo)
1492-1503	Alexander VI (Rodrigo Borgia)
1503-1513	Julius II (Giuliano della Rovere)
1513-1521	**Leo X (Giovanni de' Medici)**
1521-1523	Adrian VI (Adrian Dedel)
1523-1534	**Clement VII (Giulio de'Medici)**
1534-1549	Paul III (Alexander Farnese)
1549-1555	Julius III (de Monte)
1555	Marcellus II (Cervini)
1555-1559	Paul IV (Geanpetro Caraffa)
1559-1565	Pius IV (de' Medici)

Chapter 13

Leo X (Giovanni de' Medici)
1475-1521

L orenzo the Magnificent had three sons. His own assessment of them was that the eldest, Piero, was foolish, the second Giovanni was clever, and the youngest, Giuliano was good. But Lorenzo loved each of his sons. As they were growing up, like his grandfather Cosimo, he made it clear that no matter what affairs of the city he might be occupied with, they were always welcome to interrupt him and would receive his full attention.

Though the eldest son, Piero, succeeded Lorenzo as first citizen of Florence, he rapidly squandered the good will and prestige of the family. His foolishness in the face of the invading French army under Charles VIII led to the expulsion of the Medici and their banishment by the Council. Giovanni and Giuliano had to flee the city along with their older brother.

After Piero's death in 1503, Giovanni became the head of the Medici family. His cleverness would lead to the restoration of their political fortunes and his own elevation to a position of greater power and influence than either his father or great-grandfather.

Piero, as the eldest son, had been marked by his father for a career in business and politics. Giovanni, as the second son, was prepared for an ecclesiastical career by his parents. Giovanni's education in the classics, in the fine art of composition in classical Latin and in Greek, was intended to prepare him for the work of a high official in the church. Lorenzo's wealth and power allowed him to seek appointments for Giovanni while he was still quite young. He began to be appointed to church offices (the titles and functions remained largely honorary) when he was eight. Lorenzo used all of his diplomatic skills and influence on his son's behalf. He lobbied Pope Innocent VIII repeatedly, seeking for Giovanni the one office that would presage a powerful career within the church, the office of Cardinal.

Pope Innocent VIII was a political ally of Lorenzo, and sympathetic to his request, but he balked at naming the young Giovanni a Cardinal until he had demonstrated more maturity. Lorenzo's repeated requests finally wore him down, though. In 1489, Giovanni de' Medici, fourteen years old, was given a conditional appointment as Cardinal. Pope Innocent attached two conditions to the appointment. First, Giovanni must leave Florence and study canon law at the University of Pisa. Second, the appointment must be kept secret for a period of three years — until Giovanni had completed his studies.

In 1492, the conditions were fulfilled, and the sixteen year old Giovanni was officially invested with the office of Cardinal of the Church. As a Cardinal, or "prince of the church" Giovanni moved to Rome, to take up his duties with the College of Cardinals.

Shortly after his move to Rome, Giovanni's father Lorenzo sent him the following advice in a letter:

> "The first thing I want to impress upon you is that you ought to be grateful
> to God, remembering always that it is not through *your* merits, or *your* wis-
> dom that you have gained this dignity, but through His favor. Show your
> thankfulness by a holy, exemplary, and chaste life... You are well aware of
> how important is the example you ought to show to others as a cardinal,
> and that the world would be a better place if all cardinals were what they
> ought to be, because if they were so there would always be a good Pope and
> consequently a more peaceful world..."[13]

In 1494, the 19-year-old Giovanni was in Florence, attempting to help his older broth-er deal with the threat of the invading French army. When the people of Florence erupted in anger against Piero and the entire Medici family, Giovanni was forced to flee along with both of his brothers. The council of Florence, under the influence of Savonarola, offered a reward to anyone who would assassinate any of the three Medici brothers. Piero joined the forces of the French. Giovanni decided it would be best to depart Italy for a time. Taking his younger brother, Giulio with him, Giovanni embarked on a European grand tour that took him first to Venice, then on to Bavaria, Brussels, Rouen, Marseilles, and finally back to Genoa in Italy where they stayed with their sister Maddalena. When they returned to Rome, they were welcomed warmly by Pope Alexander VI (Roderigo Borgia) who was more and more irritated with the harsh criticisms directed at him by Savonarola and the Republic of Florence.

Giovanni settled into a palace in Rome and bided his time, enjoying the comforts of Roman society. When his elder brother Piero died in 1503, Giovanni became the head of the Medici family in exile. He strove constantly to use his influence to restore the Medici to power in Florence.

After the political and military escapades of the Borgia papacy (and the meteoric career of the Pope's son Cesare), the college of cardinals turned to the rival della Rovere family and elected Giuliano della Rovere as Pope Julius II. Cardinal Giovanni was a staunch supporter of the new Pope. Pope Julius rewarded his young supporter with commissions and offices. In his campaigns to recover for the Papacy the cities of the Papal states, he took Cardinal Giovanni along. Julius was determined not only to restore the secular power of the Papacy, but also to drive the French out of Italy. In 1512, he formed an alliance with most of the city-states of Italy (and the Spanish) and led an army northwards towards the city of Bologna which was allied with the French and garrisoned with French troops. The Republic of Florence (under the leadership of Soderini and Machiavelli) announced that they would remain neutral in the conflict, greatly displeasing Pope Julius.

The climactic battle outside Bologna between the French garrison and the troops of the Holy League, (primarily Spanish) was savage. Perhaps as many as ten thousand soldiers were killed on each side. Cardinal Giovanni was in the thick of the battle, rallying Spanish troops, mounted on horseback. The French managed to repel the attacking troops. In the aftermath of the battle, Cardinal Giovanni was taken prisoner and taken to the fortress in Bologna. Giovanni's fortunes were at their lowest ebb. Banished from Florence, impoverished by the loss of much of the family property, and now a prisoner of the French — it seemed that the head of the Medici family must soon pass into obscurity.

But Giovanni's fortunes changed rapidly in the next few months. Although the French won several more victories, each proved costly in both casualties and supplies. The French had to withdraw from Ravenna and Bologna in order to consolidate their forces and resupply their army. Then a short time later, faced with threats from both Spain and England, they withdrew from Milan and Italy completely. As the French were withdrawing, they attempted to take their valuable prisoner, Cardinal Giovanni de' Medici, with them. But at the crossing of the Po river, a band of peasants surprised the troops guarding Giovanni and in the confusion, he managed to escape.

With the withdrawal of the French, Pope Julius was free to use the Spanish and Italian troops of the Holy League against the stubbornly pro-French Republic of Florence. In August of 1512, after a short campaign, the Chancellor of the Republic, Soderini, resigned and Cardinal Giovanni de' Medici reentered the city of Florence, eighteen years after he had been forced to flee into exile.

Six months later, Pope Julius died. Cardinal Giovanni hurried from Florence to Rome to take part in the election of a new Pope. On March 11th, 1513, Giovanni de' Medici (37 years old, the second son of Lorenzo Il Magnifico) was elected Pope and took the name, Leo X. The city of Florence staged elaborate celebrations when word reached them that the head of the Medici clan had been elevated to the head of the Church.

It was a dramatic reversal of fortune. A year before he had been in exile from his home in Florence, in constrained financial straits, and a prisoner of French troops. Giovanni is reported to have said to his younger brother, "God has given us the Papacy, let us enjoy it."

Pope Leo certainly seems to have enjoyed the wealth and power bestowed upon him with his new office. He hosted a series of lavish parties, entertaining the cardinals and wealthy families of Rome. He commissioned the greatest artists in Italy to design and construct new churches and chapels in Rome and to decorate them with the finest art. He continued the papal commissions to Michelangelo, who was an old personal friend (they had been brought up together in the Medici household in Florence), though he was frustrated with Michelangelo's slow pace and stubbornness. Pope Leo also commissioned

Leonardo da Vinci to draw up plans to drain the Pontine marches. His favorite artist, though, was Raphael of Urbino.

Pope Leo prevailed upon the college of Cardinals to create Giulio de'Medici (his first cousin) a Cardinal. Leo overcame objections to Giulio's illegitimacy by appointing a committee which investigated and "discovered" that Giulio's father had secretly married his mother just before his assassination in 1478.

Pope Leo's lavish spending left him in constant need of money. To raise cash, he demanded and received large cash payments from those who wanted to be appointed as bishops or cardinals. In order to raise money, he also authorized the sale of "indulgences" — promises by the Pope to remit the penalties for sins committed on earth. The justification for this was that the "good deed" done in donating money to the church erased some of the "bad deeds" which the giver might have done. But in practice, indulgences were often promoted as simply "buying forgiveness."

In 1518, Pope Leo received a document from an Augustinian monk (and university professor) in Germany containing a series of propositions which attacked the sale of indulgences, and a number of other corrupt church practices. Luther's essay explaining the theses was dedicated to Pope Leo X. Leo X referred the matter to a minor Dominican official at the Papal Court, who penned a tract entitled *Dialogue Against the Presumptuous Theses of Martin Luther Concerning the Power of the Pope*. In this little essay, the author declared Luther's theses to be erroneous, false, presumptuous, and heretical. The tone of the writing was condescending and sarcastic. The Pope then issued a citation commanding Luther to appear in Rome within 60 days to answer for his impertinent writings. Luther, of course, never came.

In 1519, the Holy Roman Emperor Maximillian died. It was not clear who, among the many candidates, the electors of the Holy Roman Empire would choose as his successor. The favorite candidate was Maximillian's grandson, King Charles of Spain. Although Pope Leo opposed the election of Charles of Spain, in the end was unable to prevent it.

The criticisms of the Pope by Luther continued ever stronger. Pope Leo, perhaps believing that Luther could be dealt with in the same direct way as Savonarola had been, decided the time had come to condemn Luther and excommunicate him from the church.

In June, 1520, Leo issued a papal proclamation (or bull) entitled *Exurge, Domine* (from the first two words in Latin in the proclamation — "Arise O Lord"). The bull threatened Luther with excommunication, but did not take that final step. It gave Luther 60 days to recant or face excommunication.

Luther responded, when he received the proclamation from the Pope, by burning it in a public bonfire outside Wittenberg. In January of 1521, Pope Leo formally excommunicated Luther.

In April of 1521, Luther appeared before Emperor Charles V at the Imperial Diet meeting in the city of Worms. You will read more about that meeting in a later chapter.

In December of 1521 Pope Leo X died in Rome.

Chapter 14

Erasmus 1466-1536

Desiderius Erasmus was born in the Netherlands and received his early education there. He was the illegitimate son of a parish priest. As a young boy, he was sent to a school at Deventer run by the Brethren of the Common Life. The Brethren were a popular lay order, whose members were not bound by irrevocable vows. The order was designed to encourage a life of simple piety and devotion to Christ. Many of the order were also devoted to a study of the classics of Greek and Roman literature, but above all to the writings of Jerome and Augustine. Erasmus studied with the Brethren for nine years, until 1484. Erasmus' studies were brought to an end by the death of both his mother and father from the plague (in 1483 and 1484).

The churchmen who had been made guardians of both Erasmus and his older brother Peter urged them both to become monks. Although Erasmus seems not to have had any enthusiasm for monastic life, he joined the order of Augustinian priors in 1487, at the age of 21.

In 1492, at the age of 26, Erasmus was ordained a priest. Three years later, in 1495, he enrolled as a student of theology at the College de Montaigu in Paris. He did not like Paris or theology, at least as it was taught there. But he was attracted to the scholarly life and so he read the ancient classical authors and wrote essays imitating them. His years of study with the Brethren of the Common Life had given him a mastery of Ciceronian, classical Latin, and his skill as a writer was evident at an early age.

In 1499, at the age of 33, he went to England as the tutor to a nobleman's son and spent two months studying at Oxford. While in England, he was befriended by John Colet and Thomas More, members of a group of scholars who had turned their attention to the study, recovery, and revival of Greek. The objects of their studies were the early Greek writings of the church fathers, and above all, the Greek text of the books of the New Testament. Encouraged by his English friends, Erasmus took up the study of Greek. In a short time, he had made himself a master of the language.

In 1501, Erasmus published the first fruits of his studies of Paul, Jerome, and Augustine — a book called the *Enchiridion*, or *The Handbook of a Christian Knight*. In this book, Erasmus urged Christians to adopt Jesus as their model and to pattern their lives upon his. The book was a modest success, but clearly showed his friends and fellow scholars that Erasmus was a writer of great ability, with a sensitive and gentle spirit.

In 1506, he traveled to Italy as tutor to the sons of the personal physician of Henry VII. He spent a year in Bologna, then went to Venice, where he worked for the publisher, Aldus Manutius. While in Rome in 1509, he received word of the death of Henry VII and the accession of Henry VIII. Erasmus had met the young prince while he was in England. Prince Hal was himself a great admirer of the Oxford scholars and thought very highly of their Dutch friend, Desiderius Erasmus. Erasmus made plans to return to England with high hopes of joining a court ruled by a King devoted to learning and piety.

When he reached England, he took up residence in the household of his good friend, Sir Thomas More. While staying with More, he wrote a series of satirical essays entitled *In Praise of Folly (Encominium Moriae)*. This is a pun at the expense of his host (to whom the book was dedicated), since in Greek, the word for "Folly" is "Moriae." In these essays, he poked fun at men, women, merchants, the gullible, the superstitious and contrasted many of the failings of priests, monks, and nuns with the simple life of Christ and his apostles. The book proved immensely popular and established Erasmus' reputation as a gifted writer and satirist — and also as a critic of many of the practices of the church.

In 1514, he moved to Basel to work with the publisher Johannes Froben. In 1516, he published a new Latin translation of the New Testament. Erasmus, as a master of classical Ciceronian Latin, was convinced that his translation was a great improvement over the Vulgate — the Latin translation done by St. Jerome in 400 AD. To demonstrate the superiority of his new Latin translation, Erasmus had the Greek text of the New

Testament published alongside his translation. Erasmus' New Testament was a masterpiece of scholarship — but its effect was not quite what he intended. His notes and suggested Latin translations were referred to and heavily relied upon in the coming decades by every major figure of the Reformation. But instead of adopting his Latin in preference to Jerome's, the reformers used his Greek text as the basis for their own translations. Luther used it when he translated the New Testament into German. Tyndale used it when he translated the New Testament into English. These uses of his New Testament made Erasmus uncomfortable.

From 1518-1521 Erasmus lived in Louvain and held an appointment as a lecturer at the University there. It was from this vantage point that he watched events unfold in Germany as another college professor's criticism of the church escalated into an international church crisis. Erasmus privately said there was much in Luther's criticism of the church that he agreed with. Yet he felt that Luther's writings were too harsh, and his stand too uncompromising. Although Erasmus might be critical of the church, he remained unwilling to break with the Pope and Bishops and join the Lutherans. It was for this reason that contemporaries quipped that Erasmus was the man who "laid the egg that Luther hatched."

Erasmus' reputation as a man of learning, a scholar of the New Testament and especially of the writings of Jerome was at its zenith. He received invitations from kings and universities, begging him to accept appointments to write and teach. He was approached on behalf of the King of England, the King of Spain, the King of France, and the Prince of Burgundy, Charles V, the future Holy Roman Emperor.

In 1524, Erasmus returned to Basel. In that same year, he yielded at last to pressures from friends in the church and wrote a treatise criticizing one of Luther's opinions. Erasmus' essay was called *On Free Will*. He was distressed by the turmoil of the Reformation which, he said, made him "a heretic to both sides." Luther responded to Erasmus' essay with a direct attack

Erasmus *by Holbein*

entitled *On the Bondage of the Will.* In his essay, Luther attacked Erasmus for his preference for peace and quiet and his unwillingness to boldly assert the truth of the Scriptures. Luther conceded that Erasmus was a more eloquent writer, but asserted that he was an overly timid theologian who shrank from the truth of the gospel when it threatened to cause him discomfort.

In 1529 the city council of Basel declared itself in favor of the Reformation and began to reform the city's churches. Erasmus left Basel for nearby Freiburg, just down the Rhine, part of the territory controlled by the Habsburgs, and still loyal to the church at Rome.

In 1535 Erasmus returned to Basel to finish an edition of the writings of Origen. In May of 1535, he received a letter from the newly elected Pope Paul III inviting him to attend a forthcoming ecumenical council of the church. Although the Pope hinted that Erasmus was quite likely to be appointed a Cardinal if he attended, Erasmus politely declined. When he died in Basel the next year, he was still at work, writing a treatise entitled *On the Purity of the Church.*

Famous Men of the
REFORMATION

T he Reformation of the sixteenth century has been called the Great Christian Revolution. The knowledge of Greek and Hebrew achieved by the scholars of the Renaissance caused men of learning to focus their attention more closely on the text of the Bible. One of the fruits of the Renaissance was that the Scriptures began to be studied much more diligently. The contrast between the plain teaching of Scripture and the practices of the Roman church troubled many a scholar. The goal of Wyclif, Hus, and Luther (and their colleagues and successors) was to reform the church by bringing it back into conformity with the Bible. Although they achieved some measure of success locally and regionally, they were disappointed that the church as a whole became splintered and was no longer unified.

Among the figures from this turbulent time, there is much to admire, and much to lament. There are examples of tremendous courage and examples of treachery, cowardice, and betrayal. The famous men of the Reformation teach us that matters of theology are critically important. Their lives also show us that secular government more often gets it wrong than right when it meddles in the affairs of the church.

As Martin Luther so eloquently expressed it in his hymn, *A Mighty Fortress is our God*:

> That Word above all earthly powers, no thanks to them abideth.
> The Spirit and the gifts are ours, through him who with us sideth.
> Let goods and kindred go, this mortal life also.
> The body they may kill, God's truth abideth still.
> His kingdom is forever.

Chapter 15

John Wyclif 1330-1384

The century John Wyclif was born into was not a good one for the church. For most of the period, church leaders were involved in scandal after scandal. The Pope and many of the bishops were more concerned with their political power than fulfilling their spiritual duties. They often seemed willing to sacrifice anything for their political success. As a result, the reputation of the papacy and the whole church suffered greatly.

In 1302, Pope Boniface VIII became involved in a dispute with the king of France over who had the right to appoint bishops and cardinals within the kingdom of France. They also quarreled over whether priests and monks were subject to the king's courts. The Pope declared "it is altogether necessary to salvation for every human creature to be subject to the Roman pontiff."

King Philip the Fair of France responded by sending troops to Rome and taking Boniface prisoner. Pope Boniface was an old man, and the stress and shock of prison life was too much for him. He died shortly after his capture.

King Philip then arranged for a loyal French cardinal to be elected Pope. Taking the name of Clement V, the new Pope promptly declared Rome to be too dangerous to live in. He left the city, moving the papal court, the church archives and offices, and the College of Cardinals to Avignon in southern France. For the next 70 years, the Popes remained in

France. Because the Pope had obviously become a servant of the French King, the papacy lost much of its prestige and its influence over the other kingdoms of Europe. The English were especially affected since they were at war with France for most of the century. Why should they listen to a Pope who was the puppet of their enemies? To make matters worse, the papal court at Avignon became infamous for its corruption. More than one contemporary critic remarked that "everything is for sale in Avignon."

We do not know many of the details of the early life of John Wyclif. He was born sometime around 1330, near the town of Wyclif-on-Tees, not far from the Scottish border. He must have shown academic promise as a child, for we know that he enrolled at Oxford University in 1345 at the age of 15. While at Oxford, Wyclif studied under the leading theologian of his day, Thomas Bradwardine. Bradwardine spent much of his time writing and teaching about the need for reform in both the doctrine and practices of the church. Chaucer describes Bradwardine as a great theologian, along with St. Augustine and Boethius, in one of his Canterbury Tales.

In 1349, Wyclif's teacher, Bradwardine was named Archbishop of Canterbury, but he died later that same year of the Plague. Wyclif stayed in Oxford, and after completing his degree there, received a post as a lecturer. His reputation as a skilled teacher and writer brought him to the attention of his superiors in the church -- eventually, even the Archbishop of Canterbury and of the officials of the crown.

In 1374, Wyclif was sent to Bruges as a part of the delegation of the King of England to negotiate with representatives of the Papacy over the matter of papal taxes. After his mission, he returned to Oxford and began the composition of two massive treatises, *On Divine Dominion* and *On Civil Dominion*. In both these works he argued that all human authority (whether in the government or in the church) is derived directly from God and is conditional on God's approval. An official whose life is marked by sin forfeits the grant of authority from God. Wyclif believed that this principle applied equally to both Kings and Popes.

In 1377, Pope Gregory XI condemned 18 propositions taken from Wyclif's treatise, *On Civil Dominion*. Pope Gregory XI also issued bulls demanding that Wyclif be arrested and imprisoned by English authorities. But Wyclif was spared arrest and imprisonment for two reasons. First, he had a powerful protector in England — John of Gaunt, Duke of Lancaster. Duke John was the nephew of King Edward III, and when King Edward died, he appointed Duke John as regent for his young grandson (only 10 when he was crowned king), Richard II. Duke John of Gaunt was Wyclif's patron and protector. Second, because of the ongoing war between England and France, no one in England was inclined to pay much attention to the orders of the "French" Pope at Avignon.

Wyclif continued to write and teach at Oxford. He was greatly troubled by the great Schism which occurred in 1378. Pope Gregory XI had finally returned the papacy to Rome, only to die shortly after taking up residence there. The college of cardinals elected a successor, Pope Urban IV, but he was very unpopular with the French Cardinals. They withdrew from Rome and elected one of their members as Pope Clement VII who moved back to Avignon. Now, there were two Popes, one in Rome, and one in Avignon.

Partly in response to these developments, Wyclif wrote two more treatises, *On the Church*, and *On the Office of King*. In these books, Wyclif sought to return the church to standards of behavior and doctrine based on the Bible. Many of his ideas were repeated and proclaimed by later reformers like Hus and Luther. Among other things, Wyclif wrote "The church is not composed of the clergy only, but is defined as the community of all believers." Wyclif further asserted that it was entirely possible that someone might be ordained a priest, a bishop, or even a Pope and yet not be a believer, and thus, not part of the true church.

In 1378, Wyclif began to reexamine the teachings of the church on the nature of communion (also sometimes called the Eucharist, the Mass, or the Sacrament of the Lord's Supper). Wyclif concluded his examination by rejecting the teaching of the church that Jesus' body and blood were physically present in the elements of bread and wine. He argued that the bread and wine remained bread and wine (in contrast to the teaching of the church called transubstantiation — that the bread and wine literally became Jesus' flesh and blood). This break with church teaching was so radical that many of his followers deserted him.

In 1381, the peasants revolted in England. Many of them looked to Wyclif for support and encouragement. They quoted his criticisms of the corruption of the church and the government. But Wyclif did not join the peasants. He was sympathetic with the complaints of the peasants, but he did not agree with them that the King and nobles in England had been so sinful that they had forfeited their authority.

In 1382, the new Archbishop of Canterbury, Courtenay secured the condemnation by Rome of a number of Wyclif's opinions as heretical. He used the papal pronouncement to have Wyclif and a number of his followers expelled from Oxford. Wyclif returned to his position as the parish priest at Lutterworth. While in Lutterworth, he began to translate the Bible into English. He was convinced that farmers and townspeople of England needed the Bible in their own language. He also commissioned lay preachers, whom he trained to preach the simple message of the gospel. These lay preachers took portions of the Bible in English with them and encouraged those who were interested to write out copies and to meet together to read and study the Bible.

Wyclif's exile from Oxford was short, but in that time he accomplished a great deal. He died peacefully, in his sleep, in 1384.

The expulsion of Wyclif and his followers from Oxford meant that his ideas were spread throughout England. After his death, Wyclif's followers persisted as a secret, underground movement in England, carefully circulating hand-copied manuscripts of the Bible in English for over 140 years. With the coming of the Reformation, they became the first enthusiastic supporters of the ideas of Martin Luther when his writings from Germany reached English shores.

Wyclif Reading his Translation of the New Testament to his Protector- John of Gaunt, *by Ford Madox Brown, 1847-48*

Chapter 16

Jan Hus 1374-1415

Prague, in the late Middle Ages, was the intellectual capital of central Europe. It was the capital of Bohemia and the University of Prague had an international reputation. There were close connections between the Kings of Bohemia and the Kings of England. Anne of Bohemia, the sister of Wenceslaus IV (King of Bohemia, 1378-1419; Holy Roman Emperor, 1378-1400) was married to Richard II of England. Because of this close connection between England and Bohemia, John Wyclif's writings were quickly transmitted to Prague where they caused quite a stir at the University.

One of the most promising students at the University in Prague was Jan Hus. In 1393, Jan Hus had received his bachelor of arts degree from Charles University in Prague. By 1397, he had an appointment as a lecturer in the faculty of arts. Three years later, at the age of 31, Jan Hus was ordained as a priest. The next year, in 1401, he was appointed chaplain-confessor to Sophie, Queen of Bohemia.

In 1403, the views of John Wyclif were formally and publicly debated at Charles University in Prague and then condemned by a majority of the faculty. Jan Hus was one of the few members of the faculty who voted against their condemnation.

In 1409, Jan Hus was elected rector of the university (its highest office). About the same time, he received an unusual appointment as preacher at a small "people's church" called Bethlehem Chapel in Prague. This chapel had been built by a group of businessmen. After building the chapel, they each contributed money to a fund which paid to hire a preacher who was required to preach sermons, not in Latin (or in German), but in the Czech language — the language of the people.

As Jan Hus prepared sermons for the pulpit at Bethlehem Chapel and as he prepared for his lectures at the university, he found himself strongly attracted to the views of John Wyclif. In particular, he was encouraged and emboldened by Wyclif's view that the Bible, as well as the prayers and readings at the worship services, ought to be in the language of the people. He also believed strongly that both the bread **and** the cup should be given to all. It was the practice of the late medieval church to give only the consecrated bread to the people during communion. Drinking the consecrated wine was reserved for the priests only. Hus made other innovations in the worship services at Bethlehem Chapel. One of the hallmarks of his service was the singing of Czech hymns, some of which Hus composed himself.

In 1410, the archbishop of Prague ordered all of Wyclif's writings to be burned. Hus refused to condemn the Englishman. Because of his refusal, Hus was excommunicated. The archbishop also sent a report to the Pope at Rome about this recalcitrant professor and popular preacher. Pope Gregory XII summoned Hus to Rome to answer the charges against him. Hus refused to go. King Wenceslaus and Queen Sophie of Bohemia protected Hus in his refusal to go to Rome.

In 1415, Emperor Sigismund, the brother of King Wenceslaus, summoned a church council at Constance in 1415. The council was called largely to deal with the scandal of the great schism which had occurred in the church. Since 1378, there had been two Pope's, one in Rome, and one at Avignon in France. The Emperor had been encouraged by bishops and archbishops throughout the empire to summon a council to deal with the situation and determine, once and for all, who was the legitimate Pope.

The case of Jan Hus was also referred to the Council. Hus was summoned to appear, but given a safe-conduct by the Emperor -- a promise that he would not be arrested and would be allowed to return home after appearing before the Council. While in Constance, Hus wrote a defense of his views. He concluded by stating, "What Wyclif taught of truth, that I accept, not because it is the truth of Wyclif, but the truth of Christ. Four weeks after he arrived in Constance, Hus was summoned for a preliminary hearing before the Council. When he refused to renounce his books and errors, he was throne into prison. The Council declared that the safe-conduct promise of the Emperor was not valid, since Hus was obviously a heretic.

While Hus was in prison, the Council of Constance dealt with other matters of theology. It renewed the condemnation of Wyclif pronounced by the Archbishop of Canterbury and confirmed by the Pope. Since Wyclif had never recanted his views, authorities in England were instructed to remove his body from the church cemetery in which it was buried and to burn it. Next, the Council summoned Hus from prison and called on him to renounce the teachings of John Wyclif and his own innovations in preaching and worship. Hus was tired, weak, and ill from three months of imprisonment, but he refused to recant. The Council members began shouting at him. Hus waited until they were quiet and then declared, "I will gladly recant anything I have said or written which is proved untrue by the Scriptures, but I cannot recant that which agrees with Scripture.." The Council sent him back to prison.

When the Council summoned Hus next, it was to condemn him as a heretic. He was stripped of all his church offices and taken outside the city walls under armed guard and burned at the stake on July 6th, 1415. As the fire was lit, Hus began singing one of the Czech hymns he had composed for his congregation at the Bethlehem Chapel.

The Czech people were outraged. They refused to recognize Sigismund as the successor to Wenceslaus as King of Bohemia. Bohemia erupted in a civil war which raged for sixteen years. The Czech/Bohemian rebels were never defeated, but finally agreed to a truce in which their rights to receive communion in both kinds was recognized. The followers of Hus continued to exist through the years of the Reformation, Counter-Reformation, and religious wars. They are known today as the Moravian Church. Jan Hus continues to be a symbol of the fierce independence of the Czech people. Bethlehem Chapel has been restored and stands as a monument to his preaching and reform efforts. There is also a monument to Jan Hus in the town square at the center of Prague, in front of the Cathedral. During the 1968 and 1989 uprisings against Communist rule, defenders of Czech independence rallied in the square at the statue of Jan Hus. The date of his execution, July 6th, is now celebrated as a national Holiday

"I have been teaching all that Jan Hus taught — unawares, and so has Staupitz. In short, we are all Hussites, though we have not known it, even Paul and Augustine."

The exececution of Hus

Chapter 17

Martin Luther 1483-1542

At the close of the 15th century, in the small town of Mansfeld in central Germany, there lived a prosperous, middle-class family. Hans Luther had, by hard work, progressed from the status of miner, working in the copper pits, to the more respectable position of mine-owner. On November 10th, 1483, Margaret Luther, his wife, gave birth to their second child, a son, whom they named Martin.

The relative prosperity of Martin's parents meant that unlike most boys his age, he was sent to school. In 1490, at the age of seven, he began attending the Latin school at Mansfeld. In 1497, at the age of fourteen, he entered the Cathedral School in Magdeburg. After a year at Magdeburg, he moved to a school at Eisenach, where most of his mother's family lived.

In 1501, 18 years old, he enrolled at the University of Erfurt. His fellow students nicknamed him "the philosopher," the way 20th century students might call one of their classmates "the brain." One year later, he finished the traditional Arts course and received his Bachelor's Degree. In 1505, at the age of 22, Luther received his Master's Degree, placing 2nd out of 17 students. His father paid for a printed set of the Corpus Juris. This series of books (the Body of the Law), is a systematic summary of all of Roman law which had been compiled by the Emperor Justinian in 500 AD. In 1500, it was the basic reference set for anyone in the legal profession anywhere in Europe. Luther enrolled in the law school, intending to study for his doctorate. With a degree in law, he might have led a career as a public official in one of the towns of Saxony. He might have entered the service of the Elector of Saxony as a notary, or perhaps stayed at the university to teach others about the intricacies of the law. Which path he might take could be decided later, after he finished his degree. But before his study of the law was even begun, he made a sudden, dramatic change in the course of his life.

On July 17th, 1505, Luther presented himself at the Augustinian monastery in Erfurt and asked to be admitted and to be allowed to take vows of a monk. What had happened to "the philosopher?" Early in July, he had been out riding alone, and been caught in one of central Europe's rare, violent thunderstorms. The storm raged so violently, that Luther feared for his life. In terror, he called out, "Help me St. Anne, I will become a monk!"

After the storm passed, he returned to Erfurt, and promptly sold all of his expensive law books. Two weeks later, after a farewell meal with his university friends, he presented himself at the monastery. Once inside the monastery, he exchanged his "worldly" clothing for a monk's habit. After a year on probation as a novice (standard for all those considering the monastic life), he took his permanent, lifelong vows in September of 1506.

The young, former university scholar impressed his 50 brothers at the monastery. The Vicar General of all the Augustinians in Germany, who resided at the monastery in Erfurt, was particularly impressed. His name was Johannes Staupitz. His observation of young brother Martin convinced him that the former law student had great potential for service within the order. Accordingly, Luther was assigned to study theology and was ordained a priest in April, 1507. Celebrating his first mass was a great occasion. A celebration feast was held after the service and his friends and family attended. He was 24 years old. Shortly thereafter, Luther was sent back to the University of Erfurt, this time to study Theology.

In 1508, Luther was sent by his order to the small town of Wittenberg, where he was assigned to fill in as a visiting lecturer on Aristotle's *Ethics*. Vicar Staupitz continued his interest in Luther. He decided that Luther showed such academic promise that he should study for the degree of Doctor of Theology. It is possible that Staupitz was grooming Luther to be his own successor in the Chair of Theology at the University of Wittenberg.

Luther was a diligent student (and by all accounts a monk of unblemished reputation). On October 19th, 1512, at the age of 28, he was invested with the title of Doctor of Theology by the University of Erfurt. Staupitz and the Augustinian order assigned him to a position as Lecturer on the Bible at the University of Wittenberg. For the next 30 years, he continued (with only a few interruptions) as a professor, giving two lectures a week on various books of the Old and New Testament to successive generations of students. In between lectures, his outside activities led to an international crisis in the church — what we now call the Protestant Reformation.

In addition to being a university graduate, law school drop-out, Augustinian monk, and university professor, Luther was also a preacher and administrator. Since 1511, he had been preaching to his fellow monks in the Augustinian Monastery. In May of 1512, he was made sub-prior and regent of the monastery school. In 1514, he was assigned by the order to the regular task of preaching to the townspeople in the parish church of Wittenberg. His various duties kept him very busy. He described his daily activities in a letter to a friend in May, 1515:

> "I do almost nothing but letters all day long ... I am conventual preacher, reader at meals, sought for to preach daily in the parish church, am regent of studies, district Vicar (i.e. eleven times Prior), inspect the fish ponds at Leitzkau, act in the Herzberg affair at Torgau, lecture on St. Paul, revising my Psalms, ... I seldom have time to go through my canonical hours properly, or to celebrate the Mass, to say nothing of my own temptations from the world, the flesh, and the devil. You see what a lazy fellow I am."[18]

Into the world of the busy professor, monk, and town preacher, the problems of the Church and its finances (and corruption) began to intrude. In 1517, in the vicinity of Wittenberg, a traveling preacher appeared, offering to sell "indulgences" to the townspeople. An "indulgence" was a grant by the pope of forgiveness of certain of the penalties for sins.

During the Middle Ages, the Popes had decreed that participating in a church-sponsored project (such as taking part in a crusade to defend Christian pilgrims in the holy land) might be substituted for the acts of contrition and penance imposed by a priest or church court upon a repentant sinner. Then the Popes modified this arrangement to say that one did not have to personally participate, but could instead give money — and it would be considered the same as personal participation — as a substitute for the good deeds required for contrition and penance. Even this arrangement was further corrupted, however.

The "indulgence" preachers proclaimed that not only would the gift of money release one from acts of penance imposed by the church but would actually free one from any punishment which might be imposed by God because of past sins! Thus the transaction had evolved into a crude exchange of money for a piece of paper that promised complete forgiveness of the penalties (both on earth and after death) of sin. The indulgence sellers proclaimed that you could buy forgiveness not only for yourself, but also on behalf of any of your dead loved ones who might be suffering in purgatory. "As soon as the money clinks in the chest, the imprisoned soul flies to its rest." Luther, the town pastor, was appalled at what members of his congregation told him was being proclaimed by the indulgence sellers. Luther, the university theologian, was outraged at this perversion of the message of salvation taught in the Bible. Luther the monk knew that the church to whom he had sworn obedience was in serious need of reform. He decided to speak out against the false teaching of the indulgence sellers.

Why were indulgences being sold in Germany in 1517? In 1513, Pope Leo X had appointed Albert of Brandenburg Archbishop of Magdeburg. In 1514, Pope Leo also named him Archbishop of Mainz. Enormous fees were due to the Pope for these honors and Albert had to borrow money to pay them. Albert found that he owed more than he could pay. Albert's solution was to authorize (in partnership with the Pope) the sale of indulgences in his territory. In his proclamation, the Archbishop declared that the indulgences were to raise money for the building of St. Peter's cathedral in Rome. In reality, the Archbishop split the money with the Pope. Half might go for the building of St. Peters, but the other half went to Archbishop Albert who used it to pay back his huge loans.

Luther, the university professor, decided that all of the issues associated with the false teaching of the indulgence sellers needed a thorough airing and public debate. He planned to have a university-sponsored forum on the topic and in preparation, drew up a list of 95 points that should be debated and considered. On October 31st, 1517, Luther posted these debating points, the "95 Theses" on the bulletin board at the college church. Within 6 months, they were translated from Latin into German and widely distributed throughout Germany. He also sent a copy, along with a respectful letter to the Archbishop of Mainz. The Archbishop forwarded the documents to Rome, without bothering to reply to the upstart monk, Professor Luther of Wittenberg.

In early 1518, the Dominicans in Germany (who had charge of the sale and preaching of the Indulgences) charged Luther with heresy. In April of 1518, the Augustinian order held a convocation in Heidelberg. Luther attended and presided over a theological disputation on various topics, including the extent to which Aristotle's opinions should influence church teaching. Luther felt that the Bible, not philosophy should be the only thing that shaped church teaching. He would have liked to ban Aristotle from the university and theology altogether! Many in the audience were very impressed by Luther and won to his cause (Martin Bucer, a young Dominican monk, among them).

In May of 1518, Luther sent a copy of his resolutions to Pope Leo X. He also sent a letter of humble appeal, begging the Pope to use his position and authority to halt the false teaching of the indulgence sellers.

In Rome, the matter was referred to the papal court theologian, a Dominican monk called Prierias. Giovanni de' Medici (Pope Leo X) was not interested in the details of the case nor did he perceive that it was of great importance. Prierias wrote a treatise which condemned Luther and his criticisms of the church outright. He declared that it was as heretical to criticize the actions of the church as it was to criticize its teaching! Along with Prierias' pamphlet, the Pope issued a summons to Dr. Luther ordering him to appear in Rome for questioning within sixty days. Before the sixty days had elapsed, further orders were issued to both the papal representative in Germany and to the head of the Augustinian order in Saxony to have Luther arrested and sent to Rome, bound.

But Luther was not arrested. Frederick, the Elector of Saxony, protected him. Though the Elector may not have understood or especially sympathized with Luther's critique of indulgences, he had long had a high regard for Professor Martin Luther. Everyone at his court told him Luther was a fine learned fellow — not one given to heresy. In addition, the University of Wittenberg was his home town university. He was its principal sponsor. He also felt a natural, patriotic sympathy for the cause of a German monk attacked by the Italian princes of the church.

With the protection and support of the Elector, Luther refused to comply with the summons to Rome. The Pope's representative was unable to arrest Luther so long as he was protected by Frederick. The Augustinians were certainly not interested in handing over one of their most prominent members to the church courts staffed and controlled by their rivals, the Dominicans. The Pope was reluctant to challenge Frederick of Saxony directly. The Elector was an important figure in European politics and the Pope needed his help in several matters -- including the upcoming election to determine which of the German princes would be the next Holy Roman Emperor, the ruler of all of Germany.

Frederick of Saxony

In an effort to find some compromise, the Pope agreed to transfer Luther's case from Rome to Augsburg, Germany where it would be heard by the Pope's legate, Cardinal Cajetan. There was even a hint that if Luther could be persuaded to moderate his public criticisms of the Indulgences and other church practices, he might receive an appointment to the college of cardinals! Luther seems to have been unaware of all the political maneuvering around his case. He only knew that he had been charged with heresy and summoned to appear before the Papal legate in Augsburg. He went to Augsburg in October of 1518, fully expecting to be condemned as a heretic and to die a martyr's death.

The interview did not go well. Cardinal Cajetan refused to discuss or debate any of Luther's positions, but demanded again and again that he recant and submit to the authority of the church. Luther stubbornly refused and demanded that the Cardinal show him, using scripture and logic, where his opinions and writings were in error.

In spite of his fears, Luther was neither condemned nor imprisoned. The Pope was unwilling to offend Frederick of Saxony, and so, Luther returned safely from Augsburg to Wittenberg. There he waited for the blow to fall. His refusal to recant or withdraw his opinions placed him in defiance of the church. He was bitterly disappointed at the treatment of his writings by the officials of the church. He had hoped that, because his criticisms were firmly grounded in the teaching of the Bible, church officials would recognize the errors of the indulgence preachers and likewise condemn them. Now Luther began to fear that the officials of the church would never change their opinions. He knew from his study of the Bible that much of what the church taught in the matter of salvation was in error. He had seen plainly in the writings of Paul that salvation came by faith alone — "the just shall live by faith" — and that man could never do enough good works to merit God's grace. He had found that his understanding of the Bible was confirmed in the writings of St. Augustine and many others of the church fathers. He couldn't understand why the officials of the church refused to acknowledge the plain teaching of scripture.

In January of 1519, the Holy Roman Emperor Maximillian died. The scramble over who the Electors would choose to succeed him pushed the case of Dr. Luther into the background. On June 28th, 1519, Charles V, the grandson of the Emperor Maximillian of Germany and Mary of Burgundy and Ferdinand and Isabella of Spain was elected Holy Roman Emperor. You will read more about him in the next chapter. His coronation however, was postponed for over a year, until October of 1520.

In the late Spring of 1519, at the close of the academic year in Wittenberg, Luther received a letter. The letter challenged him to a debate on the topic of indulgences and church authority with Professor Eck of Ingolstadt University. The debate was held in Leipzig (in the South of Saxony) in July of 1519. Early in the debate, Dr. Eck charged that Luther was simply repeating the condemned opinions of Jan Hus. By charging that Luther was a Hussite, Dr. Eck hoped not only to associate his opponent with a condemned heretic, but also to sway public opinion against Luther. The Hussite armies had invaded and sacked a number of towns in lower Saxony in the 1400's, and Hus was not popular with the Saxons. Luther did not at first respond to the charge, but spent several days reading the writings of Jan Hus. He then came back to the debate and calmly announced that Dr. Eck was right, he was a Hussite. Luther then went further and said that he found the decrees of the Popes and Councils which condemned Hus to be in error. Dr. Eck and the audience were shocked, but Luther adamantly defended his conclusions.

By the end of 1519, the Pope's patience with Luther must have been running out. In June of 1520, with Luther having given no indication that he would change or withdraw any of his opinions, Pope Leo published the bull, Exurge domine, which declared Luther's writings to be heretical on forty-one separate points. Luther was given sixty days in which to recant or face excommunication from the church.

Luther was certainly not intimidated by the Pope. Far from withdrawing or softening any of his criticisms of the church, he broadened his charges. In August of 1520, Luther wrote An Open Letter to the Christian Nobility of the German Nation concerning the Reform of the Christian Estate in German. In October, he wrote On the Babylonian Captivity of the Church in Latin. In November, he wrote The Freedom of a Christian in Latin. In December of 1520, a group of students gathered with Dr. Luther just outside the walls of Wittenberg and burned copies of the Papal Bull which had threatened Luther with excommunication.

On January 3rd, 1521, Pope Leo X formally excommunicated Luther. Now it was up to the new Emperor, Charles V, just twenty years old, to enforce the ban of excommunication and execute the heretic, Martin Luther.

In March of 1521, the Imperial Herald arrived in Wittenberg with a summons for Luther to appear before Emperor Charles V at his first assembly of the representatives of the German nation (called a Diet) in the city of Worms (pronounced Vurms) in south central Germany. That is why this meeting is referred to as the Diet of Worms. It has nothing to do with weight loss and nutrition.

In April of 1521, Luther traveled to Worms, with warm crowds greeting him and encouraging him all along the way. In the three and a half years since his initial university forum on the topic of Indulgences, his fame had spread throughout Germany. In his subsequent writings, he had broadened and deepened his criticisms of both the theology, and the practical abuses of the church. Luther's name was on everyone's lips.

In spite of the acclamation of the crowds, Luther once again feared for his life. He knew that Jan Hus had been promised a safe conduct by the Emperor almost exactly 100 years before to attend the Council of Constance. But that safe conduct had been ignored and Hus had been arrested, imprisoned and burned at the stake in spite of the promises of the Emperor that he would be allowed to return home in safety.

Luther was asked, before the assembled nobles and the young Emperor, whether he acknowledged writing an impressive stack of books assembled as "exhibit A" and whether he was willing to retract and recall them. He surprised everyone by asking for twenty-four hours in which to consider his reply.

When he returned the next day, he said:

> "Unless I am proved wrong by the testimony of Scriptures or by evident reason I am bound in conscience and held fast to the Word of God... therefore I cannot and will not retract anything, for it is neither safe nor salutary to act against one's conscience. Here I stand. I can do no other. God help me. Amen."[19]

The twenty-year-old Emperor Charles V was not impressed and muttered, "He will not make a heretic out of me!" Though Luther was allowed to depart in peace, the Emperor drafted and had the Diet approve a decree that declared that Luther was an obstinate schismatic and manifest heretic. The decree made Luther an outlaw, subject to arrest and execution by any of the civil authorities in the Empire.

On the evening of May 4th, 1521, a small party of armed men on horseback surrounded Luther's party as it journeyed home towards Wittenberg. Everyone fled for the surrounding woods and when they returned, Luther was gone.

Albrecht Dürer, the artist, and many others were thrown into despair when they heard the news. They feared that Luther had been murdered by authorities who took the pronouncements of the Emperor and the Diet seriously.

But Luther was not dead. The attack had been arranged by Frederick of Saxony himself, Luther's protector. He thought it best if Dr. Luther disappeared for a time and Luther was hidden at Wartburg Castle, up the hill from the town of Eisenach. For ten months, Luther remained in hiding — on a leave of absence from his place at the University of Wittenberg. But he was not idle. During the long months, he completed a translation of all of the books of the New Testament from Greek (using the critical editions of Erasmus) into German. Later, after his return to Wittenberg, he would translate all of the books of the Old Testament from Hebrew into German. The "Luther Bible" was a tremendous literary accomplishment. It established the central German dialect (New High German) as a standard for his culture in much the same way that the later King James Version did for Shakespearean English.

Luther returned to Wittenberg in 1522, not because things had cooled off, but because they had heated up. With Luther in defiance of the church hierarchy and the Elector protecting him, others took advantage to proclaim their own view of the way in which the church should be reformed. Some began to talk of communism in property and in wives. Luther hurried home and preached a series of sermons in which he exhorted the townspeople to remember that no "private revelation" could be trusted unless it was in agreement with scripture.

In 1522-23 came the Knights War. The leader of the German Knights, Franz von Sickingen, proclaimed himself a follower of Dr. Luther and laid siege to the Archbishopric of Trier. He declared that he would free it from the tyranny of priestly rule. He invited Luther to join him, but Luther wisely refused. After a brief attempt to besiege the city, von Sickingen and the Knights were defeated, and von Sickingen was killed.

The next year, 1524, a series of peasant revolts began at almost the same time in dozens of villages in central and southern Germany. Many of the peasants, like von Sickingen, claimed to be followers of Luther. The peasants rose up against their masters — sometimes noblemen and sometimes priests and bishops. The peasants demanded a reduction in taxes and feudal levies, rents, and services. But in addition to their economic grievances, they also asked for the right to name their own pastors and for a return to traditional Germanic law in place of new and arbitrary changes in the law (usually based on the Roman law codes which were being imposed by the Emperor). Luther was at first sympathetic to the goals of the peasants and wrote An Appeal to Keep the Peace which called on both sides to refrain from violence and urged the nobles (including the "blind bishops and mad priests and monks") to recognize the legitimacy of much of what the peasants were asking for. Neither side was persuaded to compromise by Luther's little tract. The peasant rebellion spread to more villages and territories. In many areas, the peasants summarily executed their masters, often massacring whole families. Luther lost his temper and urged the princes to use any and all means necessary to subdue the rebellion. In late 1525, an army led by the princes of both Saxony and Hesse confronted a band of 10,000 peasants armed mostly with farming tools. The battle quickly turned into a slaughter, and 5,000 peasants were killed. Many more were executed after being captured. The leader of the peasants, Thomas Müntzer was captured, and executed. You will read more about him in the next chapter.

In June of 1525, Luther married. He had long been critical of the vows of celibacy that the church required of monks and priests. Many monks and nuns, under the influence of his teaching were leaving the monasteries. Women who left their nunneries faced immense difficulties. Luther and the other reform leaders did what they could to find them homes and whenever possible to arrange marriages for them. In 1523, twelve nuns who had escaped from their cloister arrived in Wittenberg. Several were young enough to be returned to their families. Marriages were arranged for all the others except one, Katarina von Bora. She waited patiently, serving as a servant with a Wittenberg family for two years. One prospect fell through when his family objected. Another suitor was rejected by Katarina herself. Finally, she told Luther, jokingly, that she was not trying to be unreasonable. She would consent to marriage with Dr. Luther if he proposed. Luther laughed at first, but then began to take her suggestion seriously. In June of 1525, they were betrothed and married. She was 26, he was 42. Luther said he had three reasons for marrying, to please his father, to spite the pope and the devil, and to seal his own

Katarina von Bora *by Lucas Cranach*

witness about the honorable estate of marriage. He invited one friend by writing, "You must come to my wedding. I have made the angels laugh and the devils weep."[20] To another friend he wrote, "I am to be married on Thursday. My Lord Katie and I invite you to send a barrel of the best Torgau beer, and if it is not good, you will have to drink it all yourself!"[21] The Elector of Saxony gave Martin and Katie the now abandoned Augustinian monastery as a wedding present and doubled Luther's salary from the University.

Katie brought some order to Martin's domestic life. Luther had been living in the monastery all alone. With all the other monks gone, he made use of the space in a curious fashion. When his cell needed cleaning, he simply moved down the hall to the next one.

Katie took over managing the house and quickly straightened things out. Katie soon made use of the extra rooms in the monastery by taking in student boarders. She also persuaded Martin to purchase a small farm outside of Wittenberg, at Zulsdorf. One of his letters to her is addressed, "to my beloved wife Katherine, Mrs. Dr. Luther, mistress of the pig market, lady of Zulsdorf, and whatsoever other titles may befit thy grace."[22]

Martin and Katie had six children — three sons and three daughters. One daughter died in infancy (eight months old), and another when she was thirteen, causing her father to weep great tears of grief. The eldest son, Johannes (or Hans, after his grandfather) grew up to be a lawyer and an official at the Saxon court in Weimar. Martin, the second son, studied theology, but never took a position as pastor, and died relatively young, age 33 while still living in Wittenberg. The youngest son, Paul, became a physician and eventually took a post as court physician to the elector of Brandenburg. Martin and Katie's youngest child, Margaret, married a Brandenburg nobleman and lived near her older brother, Paul.

Martin and Katie were affectionate parents. Luther once wrote to a friend, "Hans is cutting his teeth and beginning to make a joyous nuisance of himself. These are the joys of marriage of which the pope is not worthy."[23] After the birth of his daughter, Luther wrote a friend, "Dear lady, God has produced from me and my wife Katie a little heathen. We hope you will be willing to become her spiritual mother and help make her a Christian."[24]

Luther loved music and played both the lute and the flute, composing both tune and verses to a number of hymns. His most well-known composition is *A Mighty Fortress is our God*.

In spite of the threats of the Pope and Emperor, Luther continued to teach, write, and offer advice to the German princes. The Holy Roman Emperor, Charles V, was distracted by his wars with the French, the pope, and the Turks. He never seems to have really understood the depth of the convictions of Luther and his followers. He tried many times to enforce the edict of Worms against the heretic Luther and his followers, but was always prevented by the Protestant Princes of Germany (Saxony, Brandenburg, Hesse, and Anhalt) who sided with Luther .

Luther spent much of the 1530's concerned with the affairs of the University of Wittenberg, and in teaching his classes on the Bible. He was called upon for advice (both theological and political) by the princes of Germany in their efforts to reform the church and to come to some accommodation with the Emperor. Because the Emperor had other concerns and challenges, open civil war was avoided again and again.

By 1540, Luther was no longer in the best of health. He was beset with kidney stones and gallstones. He continued to lecture, and to write, but he traveled less and less. As he passed from his 50's into his 60's it was clear that he did not have long to live. Nevertheless, in 1546, he undertook a trip to mediate between two noblemen, both counts of Mansfeld in his hometown of Eisleben. While there, he appeared to suffer a series of heart attacks but then seemed to recover. After successfully reconciling the feuding parties, he fell ill again and died on February 18th, 1546.

Luther was at times modest about his own role in reforming the church. He insisted that God and his Word should have the credit, as he wrote to a friend,

"I simply taught, preached, wrote God's Word: otherwise I did nothing. And then, while I slept or drank Wittenberg beer with my Philip and my Amsdorf, the Word so greatly weakened the Papacy that never a Prince or Emperor inflicted such damage upon it. I did nothing. The Word did it all. Had I desired to foment trouble, I could have brought such a little game at Worms, that the Emperor would not have been safe. But what would it have been? A mug's game. I left it to the Word."[25]

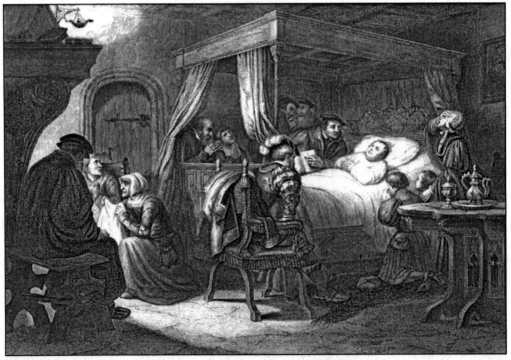

Luther's death

Chapter 18

Charles V 1500-1558

Young Prince Charles was the son of Philip the Fair and the grandson of Emperor Maximillian and Mary of Burgundy. From his paternal grandfather, he inherited a claim to the title of Holy Roman Emperor (though this had to be confirmed by the seven Imperial electors) and the lands of the Habsburg family in Austria. From his paternal grandmother, he inherited Burgundy — a collection of territories between France and Germany, the wealthiest portion of them make up the modern day countries of Belgium and Holland.

His mother was Joanna of Spain. His maternal grandparents were Ferdinand of Aragon and Isabella of Castile. Combining the kingdoms of Aragon and Castile, he became Charles I, the first king of a united Spain. Through his four grandparents he had inherited lands and titles that made him ruler of a kingdom the size of Charlemagne's empire. The domains of Julius Caesar and Alexander the Great were not much more impressive.

Charles was born in Ghent on February 24, 1500. While he was still an infant, his parents moved to Spain and left him in the Netherlands in the care of one of his aunts, Margaret of York, the widow of Duke Charles the Bold of Burgundy. When he was seven, his father died and he inherited the first of his titles, Duke of Burgundy. Since he was too young to rule in his own name, another of his aunts, Margaret of Austria, moved to the Netherlands as regent and governess for the young prince.

Charles was educated by a succession of private tutors at the home of the Dukes of Burgundy. One of his tutors was Adrian of Utrecht, a northern humanist and colleague of Erasmus of Rotterdam. Adrian was also a churchman who served as a priest and bishop. In 1517, he was elected to the college of Cardinals. When Pope Leo X died in 1521, Charles' tutor was elected Pope Adrian VI. He was the last non-Italian Pope until the election of the Polish Cardinal Karol Wojtyla as Pope John Paul II in 1978.

In 1515, the young Duke of Burgundy was named regent for Castile (part of modern Spain), due to his mother's mental illness (she came to be known as Joanna the Mad). When his grandfather, Ferdinand of Aragon died a year later he became ruler of all of Spain as well as all Spanish possessions in the Americas. In 1519, his other grandfather, the Emperor Maximillian died. Charles immediately launched a well-laid plan to secure for himself election as the new Emperor. He was nineteen years old.

Charles' native language was French. He never became fluent in Flemish, and he learned Spanish only after he had become king — though it was to Spain that he turned in the last years of his life when he wished to retire. He could speak no German and his Latin was poor.

Both Pope Leo X and the young king of France, Francis I (at 24, just five years older than Charles V) opposed Charles' election as Emperor. With the backing of the Pope's influence and money, Francis began his own campaign to be elected Emperor. For a time, it appeared that Frederick the Wise of Saxony would be a compromise candidate who might be acceptable to a majority of the seven electors. But Frederick had no wish to be Emperor, and in the end, he persuaded the other electors to vote for Charles V.

Between 1521 and 1559 Charles fought four wars with Francis in what came to be known as the Habsburg-Valois Wars. The initial campaigns were conducted in Northern Italy over the city of Milan. In 1525, the forces of Charles defeated Francis so thoroughly at Pavia that the French King was taken prisoner and sent to Madrid. Charles forced Francis to abandon all claims to the city-state of Milan and acknowledge the Habsburg possession of Burgundy and the Netherlands in exchange for his freedom. Francis repudiated the treaty as soon as he was freed and safely back in France.

Francis rallied his allies among the Italian city-states and gained the support of the new Pope Clement VII who felt threatened by the Habsburg presence in Italy. Clement had reason to be frightened. In 1527, Charles' imperial army (composed largely of German mercenaries) occupied Rome and then mutinied because of delays in receiving their pay. Many of the German soldiers were believed to have Lutheran sympathies and they sacked Rome with a vengeance. Churches were looted, priests and nuns molested, civilians murdered, and the Pope himself taken prisoner.

In exchange for his freedom, Charles forced the Pope to promise to call a general council of the church. Charles wanted a council to deal with the crisis caused by the persistent criticisms of Luther and his followers in Germany. Once he was free however, Pope Clement delayed the actual summoning of a council. In 1529, as Charles turned from Rome and headed back to the north of Italy, he met Francis and defeated him in a second Italian campaign. The Pope had chosen the wrong side once again. He now had no choice but to agree to Charles V's demands and crown him Holy Roman Emperor. Charles wanted to emulate Charlemagne who had been crowned by the Pope in 800 — though that ceremony took place in Bologna rather than in Rome. Charles V was the last Emperor to be crowned by the Pope.

Because Charles' territories covered such a large area, he had problems with more than just the Pope and the king of France. In 1526, a Turkish army had disastrously defeated the king of Hungary at the battle of Mohacs. In 1529, another Turkish army marched up the Danube and laid siege to Vienna. Charles V was frustrated. He had defeated the French and the Pope and was ready to turn his attention to dealing with the Lutheran princes in Germany. But now, he found that instead of being able to confront them militarily, he needed their help to face the Turkish threat. He had been absent from Germany for eight years (since the Diet of Worms in 1521), and his first business upon returning was to raise an army to relieve Vienna.

After raising the siege of Vienna, Charles returned to Germany, resolved to deal with the Lutheran controversy. A Diet was called for Augsburg in 1530. Luther himself was not permitted to attend, but his young colleague from the University of Wittenberg, Philip Melanchthon, was allowed to represent the "Protestant" cause. The group of German princes who supported Luther were called "Protestants" because they had "protested" the Emperor's announcement in 1529 that he intended to enforce the edict of Worms and compel a return to obedience to the Roman church in all his territory.

Charles V *by Titian*

Charles ignored the appeals made by the Lutheran princes and the Imperial cities and ordered all Protestant territories to return to obedience. He demanded that they reinstate the Roman Mass by April of 1531. The Protestants refused and began to prepare for war. Renewed threats from the Turks in 1531 and from France in 1536 distracted Charles from the religious problems in Germany and the issues remained unresolved.

In 1536, Francis pulled out all the stops in his assault on Charles. He had prepared carefully, first securing the support of the Pope by arranging a marriage between his son, the future Henry II and the Pope's niece, Catherine de' Medici. He then took the bold and controversial step of signing a formal alliance with the Turkish Sultan, Suleiman the Magnificent. Charles was both surprised and shocked. For the next ten years, the Christian King of France was allied with the Muslim Turks as they both fought the forces of Charles V, King of Spain, and Holy Roman Emperor.

The first French campaign ended in a stalemate in 1538. When Francis renewed hostilities in 1542, Charles assembled a large force from the German princes and his possessions in the Netherlands and invaded France. With the Imperial forces threatening Paris, Charles offered his great rival generous peace terms and Francis had no choice but to agree. Worn out from his many years as a soldier, Francis died in 1547 at the age of 52. Even with Francis dead, Charles' troubles were not over. He had 10 more years of conflict seeking to secure his far-flung possessions.

In addition to his conflicts with the king of France, Charles had to contend with the ambitions of the Turkish sultan. Suleiman had defeated the King of Hungary in 1526 and had taken the city of Budapest in 1529. His armies laid siege to Vienna in both 1529 and in 1532. There were major battles between the Spanish and Turkish fleets in the Eastern Mediterranean in 1532, near Tunis in 1535 and Algiers in 1536. Renewed operations against the Turks in Algiers in 1541 were frustrated when the French allowed the Turkish ships to use their harbors and refit over the winter, rather than being forced to return to their own ports in the East.

After Charles' victory over Francis in 1544, he was at last free to turn his attention to the dissident and disobedient princes and cities of Germany who refused to return to obedience to the church. In 1546 and 1547, Charles' armies gradually besieged and occupied the rebellious imperial cities, and then defeated the Protestant princes in April of 1547. Both the elector of Saxony (John Frederick, the son of Frederick the Wise) and the Landgraf of Hesse (the two strongest of the Protestant states) were taken prisoner. Luther had died in 1546 and when the Emperor's forces occupied Wittenberg, some of the soldiers wanted to dig Luther's body up and burn it. Charles sent word that Luther was to be allowed to rest undisturbed. "I don't make war upon dead men," Charles is reported to have said.

Charles spent his last years in semiretirement at a monastic retreat in Spain. His goal of reviving the empire of Charlemagne had largely failed, though he had kept all that he had inherited. His desire to see Germany once again united in obedience to the Pope at Rome was frustrated, in spite of his military victories over the Protestant princes. His German subjects simply refused to abandon the teachings of Luther and the other reformers, in spite of being ruled and oppressed by imperial governors.

Towards the end of his life, Charles gradually turned the rule of his Spanish kingdom and his Italian and Flemish possessions over to his son, Philip II. Charles started by naming Philip, Duke of Milan (though he never visited the city). Later he had his son proclaimed as the King of Spain. Charles' German and Austrian possessions, and his imperial title went to his younger brother, Ferdinand, who lived in Vienna.

In 1556, Charles V abdicated all of his titles in favor of his son and brother. He died in Spain, two years later.

Chapter 19

Albrecht Dürer 1471-1528

Albrecht Dürer was born in 1471, in Nuremberg, Germany. His father was a successful goldsmith. The Dürer's had 18 children, but only 3 sons survived to adulthood. Albrecht was the oldest surviving child.

Young Albrecht, as the eldest son, was expected to follow in his father's footsteps and learn the goldsmith's craft, so that he could take over the shop one day. But Albrecht soon showed both interests and talents that would take him far beyond the goldsmith's shop.

"And my father took special pleasure in me because he saw that I was diligent in striving to learn. So he sent me to the school, and when I had learned to read and write he took me away from it and taught me the goldsmith's craft. But when I could work neatly, my liking drew me more to painting than to goldsmith's work. So I put it to my father. But he was troubled, for he regretted the time lost while I had been learning to be a goldsmith. Still, he let me have my way, and in 1486, as one counts from the birth of Christ, on St. Andrew's Day, my father bound me apprentice to Michael Wolgemut, to serve him three years long. During that time God gave me diligence so that I learned well, but I had to endure much from his apprentices."[14]

One of Dürer's earliest sketches from his youth has survived. It is a self-portrait with an inscription on it which reads "I drew this myself from a mirror in the year 1484, when I was still a child. Albrecht Dürer." The drawing itself is stunning. It displays a skill in drawing which is breathtaking in one so young — just 13 years old!

Albrecht's father, recognizing his son's gift and skill in drawing, sought out for him the best master in Nuremberg to teach him the art of drawing and painting. In the workshop of Michael Wolgemut, Dürer learned quickly all of the technical skills of an artist. From Master Wolgemut he learned to paint in oils and especially the new and profitable technique of preparing woodcut illustration blocks for printed books.

At 19, having completed the years of his apprenticeship, Albrecht traveled to Frankfurt and Mainz (perhaps with a side trip to the Netherlands), then southwards, up the Rhine to Basel.

Self Portrait at 22 *by Albrecht Dürer*

Mainz and Basel were both centers of the printing industry (Gutenberg's printing press had been invented in Mainz). While in Basel, Dürer supported himself by doing drawings for woodcuts to illustrate books. After an absence of four years, the 22-year-old Dürer decided it was time to return home. One of the reasons for his return was to attend his own wedding. In his absence, his parents had arranged his betrothal to the daughter of a prominent businessman in Nuremberg. His intended bride brought with her a dowry of 200 gold florins (the price of a comfortable house in the city). Agnes Frey was 19. She became not just Albrecht's wife, but also his assistant, partner, and business manager. Albrecht created paintings, drawings, and woodcuts. Agnes arranged for their distribution and sale.

Immediately after the wedding, Albrecht set off on another trip abroad — this time to Italy. There were several unusual things about this trip. First, in his four year absence from his 18th to his 22nd year, Albrecht had completed a traditional part of his training as an artist. He had visited other workshops in Germany and learned from firsthand acquaintance what manner of style, technique, and composition were in use by his contemporaries. His second trip was unnecessary from the point of view of the traditional training of an artist.

His choice of destination — Italy — was also unusual. Before Dürer's journey south, German artists had shown little interest in Italian painters. But a number of things attracted Dürer to Italy. He had heard of the new publishing enterprise in Venice, headed by Aldus Manutius. Manutius was an Italian businessman who employed German printers and German illustrators and specialized in scholarly editions of Greek and Latin classics. He may also have seen some engravings and illustrations done by Italian artists while he was working in Basel.

Another reason for his trip to Italy was that the German Emperor Maximillian had just married for a second time, to Bianca Maria Sforza, daughter of the Duke of Milan. Since Nuremberg was a free imperial city, with close connections to the Emperor and his court, there was a heightened interest in all things Italian, because of the Emperor's pretty Italian bride. Dürer went first to Venice, where Nuremberg merchants had regular dealings and some even maintained warehouses to store goods for transport north over the Alps to Germany.

In Venice, Dürer was fascinated above all with the works of Mantegna. Mantegna was a master of perspective and foreshortening. In Mantegna, Dürer found an artist who combined all that the northern Italians had been learning about composition and color in the new style of the Renaissance. After a year in Venice (with perhaps side trips to a few other nearby cities such as Padua), Dürer returned to Nuremberg. On the return trip to Nuremberg, he met Willibald Pirckheimer, a young classical scholar, on his way home from studying at the Italian Universities of Padua and Pavia. Pirckheimer was to become the

Petrarch of the North. Like Petrarch, he had a passion for all things Greek and Roman. He personally translated hundreds of classical works — from Greek into Latin (since Greek was much less widely known than classical Latin) and from Greek and Latin into German. Pirckheimer and Dürer began a close friendship which lasted for almost 40 years.

When Dürer returned to Nuremberg in 1495, he established his own workshop. As in Basel, his specialty was in preparing illustrations for engravings and woodcuts used to illustrate that new-fangled innovation, the printed book. But rather than simply act as illustrator, Dürer established himself as publisher as well. One of his first books was an illustrated edition of the book of *Revelation*. Dürer produced a stunning set of illustrations and brought out both a Latin

The Four Horseman of the Apocalypse *by Dürer*

and a German edition. Dürer's depiction of *The Four Horseman of the Apocalypse* was widely admired and the book was a huge financial success. Dürer followed up the success of his Apocalypse illustrations with other depictions of biblical scenes.

In 1496, Dürer did an engraving of *The Prodigal Son*, which created a sensation. Rather than depict the wandering son in his sins (drinking and partying), Dürer chose to portray him at the moment of repentance when he comes to his senses after he has exhausted his resources and is reduced to feeding pigs. The illustration was widely copied throughout Europe, and even Italian artists praised it and recognized that there was now a talent to rival theirs north of the Alps.

Dürer's reputation as a skilled and sensitive illustrator of biblical themes led to commissions from wealthy merchants in Nuremberg and beyond, from German nobleman (among them, Frederic the Wise of Saxony), and from churches and monasteries.

In 1505, Dürer made a second journey to Italy. By now he was a famous artist. His prints were sold from Holland to Italy. He had his own personal sales agent who handled sales in the Italian city states. His primary purpose for the trip was once again to visit Venice. While staying there, he received a commission from the German merchants to paint an altarpiece for their chapel (the German merchants maintained their own church in Venice).

In 1509, after returning to his workshop in Nuremberg, Dürer received a commission for an altar painting for the Dominican church in Frankfurt am Main. He also continued work on engravings for publication of religious pamphlets. Some versions of these books were published with blank pages next to the woodcut illustrations so that the owner might write in his (or her) own devotional prayers. Elector Frederic the Wise of Saxony possessed a copy of one of Dürer's books on the Passion of Jesus with his own prayers inscribed in just such a fashion.

In 1512, Dürer began to compose a painter's manual, entitled, *Food for Young Artists*. In it, he summarized what he had learned about perspective, anatomy, drawing techniques, color, composition and also the business details of accepting commissions and supervising a workshop. Also in 1512 he was commissioned by the town council of Nuremberg to paint portraits of Charlemagne (Karl der Grösste) and Emperor Sigismund. When the Emperor Maximillian himself visited Nuremberg, he greatly admired the portraits, especially the one of Charlemagne.

In 1516, Dürer and his friends, Pirckheimer and Lazarus Spengler, secretary to the town council, attended a series of Advent sermons given by Johannes Staupitz, Vicar-General of the Augustinian Order in Germany. The theme of the sermons was *On True Repentance*. Staupitz was the former Dean of the Theological Faculty at Wittenberg University — the man who hired Martin Luther as a professor of Bible and Theology. Staupitz stressed God's infinite capacity for forgiveness and the Death of Jesus on the cross as the only true key to salvation. Dürer and his friends were impressed with Staupitz and his presentation of the gospel. They began to meet together to discuss and debate his sermons. The group called itself the "Staupitz Fellowship" (sodalitas Staupitziana). Staupitz returned in the spring of 1517, to preach a series of Lenten sermons in Nuremberg. The "Staupitz Fellowship" attended them eagerly and invited the Augustinian vicar to dine with them to discuss his sermons. Some months later, members of the "Staupitz Fellowship" received a copy of the 95 Theses — written by Stauptiz's student and protégé on the faculty of the University of Wittenberg, Martin Luther. Dürer was immediately impressed with Luther's writings. In 1518, he sent Luther a gift of some of his own prints. Luther responded by sending his thanks to the great German artist.

In 1520, Dürer received a gift of some of Luther's books from one of the noblemen to whom he had sold his art over the years, Frederic the Wise, Elector of Saxony. In a letter to the Elector's secretary, he wrote:

> "... I pray your honor to convey my humble gratitude to His Electoral Grace, and beg him humbly that he will protect the praiseworthy Dr. Martin Luther for the sake of Christian truth. It matters more than all the riches and power of this world, for with time everything passes away; only the truth is eternal. And if God helps me to come and visit Dr. Luther, then I will carefully draw his portrait and engrave it in copper for a lasting remembrance of this Christian man who has helped me out of great distress. And I beg you... to buy on my account, anything new that Dr. Martin may write in German."[15]

When Luther was excommunicated in 1520, the Bull named six other followers who were also excommunicated — among them were two members of the "Staupitz Fellowship" in Nuremberg, Spengler and Pirckheimer.

On January 12th, 1519, the Emperor Maximillian died. Just who his successor would be was not immediately clear. After months of wrangling and behind-the-scenes maneuvering, the electors of the Holy Roman Emperor met and elected Maximillian's grandson, King Charles of Spain as the new Emperor.

In July 1520, Dürer left Nuremberg for the Netherlands to attend the coronation of Charles V as Holy Roman Emperor. Dürer made his headquarters in Antwerp, though the coronation itself was planned for Aachen, the site of the tomb of Charlemagne. Dürer stayed in Antwerp for almost a year. He chose Antwerp for several reasons. It was a prosperous city, much like Venice. Many of the influential members of the new Emperor's court and family were to be found here. Dürer was particularly anxious to secure as much support as possible for his own petition to the new Emperor. Dürer wanted the Emperor to confirm the grant by his late grandfather, Maximillian, of a retirement pension, to be paid to Dürer by the city of Nuremberg and deducted from the taxes due by the city to the Emperor.

The civic leaders in Antwerp were pleased to host the great German artist. They hoped to persuade him to settle in their city permanently. They staged a sumptuous banquet in honor of Dürer, treating him like nobility. They offered him an annual salary and the use of a large house in the city, rent-free.

A few weeks after arriving in Antwerp, Dürer took a side trip to the cities of Mechelen and Brussels. One of his reasons for the trip was apparently to visit an exhibition of artwork brought back to Europe from the new world. Specifically, these were Aztec works, sent by Cortez (recent conqueror of Mexico City) to Charles V in his capacity as King of Spain. Dürer was fascinated by the large gold images of the sun and by the elaborate feathered costumes of the Aztec priests.

In Brussels, Dürer also met Desiderius Erasmus and sketched several portraits of him in charcoal. In October, 1520 he traveled from Antwerp to Aachen for the coronation of Charles V as Holy Roman Emperor. In November, the Emperor signed the order confirming his pension.

In his diary for these months there are several entries indicating that he purchased pamphlets by and about Martin Luther whenever he found them. In January of 1521, after his coronation in Aachen, the Emperor traveled to the German city of Worms and presided over the first assembly of the German nobility under his reign. It was to this Assembly (or Diet) that Dr. Martin Luther was summoned to explain his criticisms of the practices of the church and the Pope.

In May, 1521, Dürer, still in Antwerp received the news that Dr. Luther had been betrayed and possibly murdered during his journey home from Worms.

> "... And if we have lost this man, who has written more clearly than any that has lived for 140 years, and to whom Thou hast given such a spirit of the Gospel, we pray Thee O Heavenly Father, that Thou wouldst again give Thy Holy Spirit to another, that he may gather Thy church anew everywhere together...
>
> ... God, if Luther is dead, who will henceforth deliver the Holy Gospel to us with such clearness? Ach, God, what might he not still have written for us in ten or twenty years?... O Erasmus of Rotterdam, where will you stand?"[16]

Dürer returned to Nuremberg in July of 1521. It was clear to everyone that he was sympathetic to the teachings of Luther and the Reformers of Wittenberg. In November of 1521, Andreas Bodenstein von Karlstadt, professor of theology at the University of Wittenberg, who was leading the Reformation of the church in Wittenberg during Luther's absence, had published a pamphlet *On the Adoration and Veneration of the Symbols of the New Testament*. In his pamphlet, Karlstadt proclaimed again Luther's position that both the bread and the wine should be served to communicants, and not just the bread as had become the practice of the medieval church. The pamphlet was dedicated to Albrecht Dürer.

In 1526, Dürer completed a painting of *The Four Holy Men* (John, Peter, Mark, Paul). In this painting, St. John is holding a Bible which is opened to the first chapter of his own gospel. The words Dürer painted are in German, taken from Luther's translation of the New Testament, completed in 1522.

In 1525, Philip Melanchthon came to Nuremberg to advise the city on the reform of the church. Melanchthon also gave advice

Four Holy Men *by Dürer*

on the establishment of the first gymnasium (or high school) to be operated by the city, rather than by the church. Dürer created an engraved portrait of Melanchthon during his stay in the city.

Dürer died on April 6th, 1528, at the age of 57. Luther, Melanchthon, Erasmus, and others all sent letters of condolence to his widow and to his friends in Nuremberg.

On the left, *Self Portraits at 22, 26, and 28*. On the right, *Knight, Death, and the Devil*.

Chapter 20

Ulrich Zwingli 1484-1531

I n 1500, the area we now call Switzerland was nominally a part of the Holy Roman Empire and under the authority of the Emperor. The Swiss Confederation was composed of thirteen cantons — each one similar in size and government to an American county. The thirteen cantons in the mountains and foothills of the Alps were, for all practical purposes, politically independent. A brief attempt by the Emperor Maximillian in 1499 to force his authority on the people of the region had ended disastrously for him. Although they acknowledged Maximillian as their emperor, the Swiss were zealous guardians of their independence. Each of the cantons governed themselves and all thirteen were bound by treaty to defend the rights and privileges of each other against any aggressor, including the emperor. The Swiss supplied soldiers for hire to many of the major powers throughout Europe. Their skill on the battlefield was widely respected. The Pope and the Italian cities vied with each other in bidding for the services of Swiss mercenary companies.

Ulrich Zwingli was born in 1484, one year after Martin Luther. He grew up on a farm in a small Swiss village in the canton of St. Gall. His father was a minor local official. He attended school in both Basel and Bern. He enrolled at the University of Vienna in 1498 (three years before Luther enrolled at the University of Erfurt). Four years later, he moved to Basel and enrolled at the University there. He received a degree as master of philosophy from Basel in 1506. He had studied not only philosophy (and theology) but also the "new learning" of the humanists. He greatly admired the classical Latin style of the humanist writers and shared their interest in the recovery of both Greek and Hebrew. Rather than pursuing an academic career, however, in 1506 he left the university. He was ordained a priest, and took a post as parish priest in the little town of Glarus, chief town of the canton (roughly equivalent to an American county) of Glarus.

For ten years, Zwingli, was the parish priest in Glarus. Not only did he preach in the village church, but he found time to pursue his interest in the writings of the humanists and the church fathers. He continued his studies in Greek and also began to learn Hebrew. His studies were motivated by his desire to understand the Scriptures, and to be able to preach them to his parishioners clearly. His friends and correspondents began to refer to him as "the Cicero of our age."

When Erasmus' edition of the Greek New Testament was published in 1516, Zwingli was one of the first to purchase an edition. He studied it diligently. By all accounts, he was also a very conscientious parish priest, regularly visiting the sick, preaching and celebrating mass several times each week. He also took an interest in education and established a school for the children in his parish and was one of the teachers.

In 1513 and 1515, Zwingli traveled south from Glarus to Italy. He went as chaplain to a company of mercenary soldiers from the canton. As a result of this experience, he opposed the practice of supplying mercenary soldiers for the wars in Italy, France, & Germany. This practice had been a major component of the Swiss economy, especially in the agriculturally poor, mountainous cantons.

In 1518, the city fathers of Zurich began looking for someone to fill the post of preacher at the city church (called the Great Minster). Zwingli applied and was one of two finalists for the position. The backers of the rival candidate accused Zwingli of being of questionable moral character, since he was known to be a player of musical instruments and he had seduced the daughter of a prominent citizen in his parish in Glarus. Zwingli replied to these accusations with a straightforward acknowledgment. Yes, he was a musician, though he saw no immorality in music. And yes, he had sinned with a young woman in his parish — an act he now deeply regretted. Since Zwingli's rival was living openly with his mistress and six illegitimate children, it is not surprising that Zwingli won the election to the post by a vote of 17 to 7. He moved to Zurich in January of 1519 and, at the age of 35, assumed his post as the chief preacher of the city.

His first sermons in Zurich made a dramatic impact. The typical sermon in Europe at the time was very dry and pedantic. Preachers came in several styles, but most often, they focused on fanciful allegorical interpretations of scripture — treating it as if it were written in a secret code where everything mentioned stood as a symbol for something else. Preachers were also fond of showing off their university learning by extended quotations from the ancient and medieval theologians.

Zwingli's style was completely different. He began preaching directly from the Bible, verse by verse, explaining and commenting on the plain sense of what the Scripture said. In his first sermon, he began with the Gospel of Matthew. When he finished with the life of Jesus, he continued on with the book of Acts. It took him six years, but he eventually preached through the entire New Testament. In the pulpit, Zwingli used Erasmus' Greek text and often commented on the meaning of particular words in Greek and how they ought to be translated. The effect of the sermons was electric. The well-educated were impressed with his command of Greek and his attention to scholarly detail. The less well-educated were drawn to his clear and persuasive proclamation of the Gospel.

During his first year in Zurich, there was an outbreak of the plague. Zwingli proved his courage by refusing to flee the city. He stayed to preach and visit the sick, at great risk to himself. He became ill and nearly died.

Zwingli preached over and over again that only the Scriptures were a reliable guide to God's will and what he required from men. He challenged the citizens of Zurich to examine their lives, their business practices, and even the traditions of the church to see if they were consistent with Scripture. His preaching had great impact. In 1522, a group of influential citizens, inspired by Zwingli, decided that the fasts and regulations imposed by the church for the season of lent (the 30 days leading up to Easter Sunday) were not justified by Scripture. Accordingly, they met on Ash Wednesday, the first day of Lent, and deliberately enjoyed a meal of fried sausages — a direct violation of the church's canon law which decreed that all Christians were to abstain from meat during Lent. The city council of Zurich was scandalized and had them arrested and fined.

Zwingli preached a sermon defending their actions and had it published as a pamphlet called Concerning Choice and Freedom of Food. He made it clear that there was nothing in the Bible which prohibited Christians from eating sausages during Lent. Tension between Zwingli and the town council was high. In hopes of persuading the leaders of Zurich that his critique of church traditions was correctly based on Scripture, Zwingli suggested that he and his critics should hold a public disputation. The city council agreed and scheduled the debate for January of 1523.

In preparation for the debate, Zwingli prepared a summary of his views on Scripture and church practices called the Sixty-Seven Articles. The first sixteen of these articles stated his allegiance to the authority of the Scriptures. They explained the person and work of Jesus Christ, and asserted that believers were saved on the basis of faith and not works. Then, the remaining articles attacked what Zwingli saw as the abuses, and unbiblical, unjustified practices of the church. These included fasting, pilgrimages, monastic vows, clerical celibacy, the sale of indulgences and the doctrines of penance and purgatory. Zwingli attacked them all because they had no justification in the Bible. Zwingli saw himself and his supporters as returning the church to its original practice and teachings and purifying it from the man-made innovations of the "dark ages."

Zwingli sat at a table in the front of the hall, with his Greek, Hebrew, and Latin Bibles open in front of him. At the conclusion of the Disputation, The Council sided with Zwingli. They ordered all priests and preachers to preach from and be governed by the Scriptures.

A second disputation was held in October of 1523 primarily on the issue of the continuation of the Mass and the use of images. Once again, Zwingli challenged those who defended the current practices of the church to justify them from Scripture. At the conclusion of the second disputation, the Zurich town council once again agreed with Zwingli. They issued ordinances directing the removal of all images from churches in the city, as well as the dismantling of the church organs. Henceforth, the only music allowed was to be the singing of the Psalms. Zwingli wrote proudly to friends describing the bright, beautiful white-washed walls of the churches in Zurich now that they had been reformed according to the Scriptures.

The celebration of the Mass was ended by the town council as well. Zwingli rejected most of the Catholic teaching on the meaning and significance of the Mass. His understanding of Jesus' instructions in the New Testament was that the celebration of the Lord's Supper was intended as a memorial service, "remembering the Lord's death until he comes." He rejected the practice of distributing only the bread to the congregation. He rejected the Doctrine of Transubstantiation which taught that the bread and wine were miraculously "trans-substantiated" into the actual body and blood of Jesus. Zwingli altered the liturgy of the service so that it was no longer in Latin — a language that few could understand — but translated into German, the language of the people of Zurich.

In 1524, Zwingli announced to his congregation in Zurich that not only did he believe that the practice of clerical celibacy to be un-scriptural, but that he had acted on his belief — he had been married in 1522.

Some of Zwingli's followers were impatient with the pace of reform in the city. They thought that Zwingli had taken far too long to deal with the issue of statues and images in the churches. They also wished him to expand his critique of the practices of the Catholic church and reexamine the practice of infant baptism. This group, led by Conrad Grebel (whom you will read more about in a later chapter), believed there was no Biblical support for the baptism of infants. In 1525, they began to preach against the practice and to encourage adult believers to be re-baptized on the basis of their own personal profession of faith. Zwingli and the town council opposed Grebel and his followers and tried to forbid their preaching. When they refused to stop, they were arrested, tried and sentenced to prison. The Anabaptists (Latin for re-baptizers) were eventually driven from Zurich, though they persisted in the face of incredible persecution as a separate and usually underground church throughout Europe.

Zwingli's actions in Zurich were, for the most part, welcomed and applauded by Luther in Germany. Luther agreed and approved of Zwingli's assertion that Scripture should govern all questions of both theology and practice in the church. He agreed with Zwingli's criticism of monasticism, celibacy. Luther's marriage to Katarina von Bora occurred about 12 months after Zwingli's announcement of his own marriage. But Luther privately had reservations about the whitewashing of churches. Luther's greatest disagreement with Zwingli, though, was over the understanding of the Sacrament of Communion. Luther had himself reformed the way that the Mass was celebrated in Wittenberg. Like Zwingli, Luther too, believed that the service should be in the language of the people, (not Latin) and that there was no Scriptural justification for withholding communion in both kinds from the laity. Luther and Zwingli parted ways over the notion of whether Communion was a memorial service (as Zwingli maintained) or whether Jesus' body and blood were really and truly present in the elements (as Luther believed).

In 1526, Luther published a pamphlet criticizing Zwingli's views. In 1527, Zwingli responded with a pamphlet defending his position. Two months later, Luther fired back. Zwingli responded once again. By 1528, it was clear that neither man was going to persuade the other.

Because the Protestant princes knew Emperor Charles might turn his attention to the rooting out of heresy from among his German princes and cities at any time, various leaders attempted to reconcile Luther and Zwingli with each other. The Landgrave of Hesse (Philipp II) in particular was anxious to establish an alliance between Hesse, Saxony, and the cities of Zurich and Strasburg (among others). He persuaded leaders of the Protestant churches to meet in his castle in Marburg in 1529 in an attempt to come to agreement on basic issues of theology. Theological agreement, he hoped would lead to a political and military alliance which would protect the Protestants against the Catholic allies of the Emperor.

Luther, Zwingli, and eight other theologians met for five days and managed to draft a summary of their theology that all could agree to — almost. They drew up fourteen points covering such issues as salvation by faith alone and the authority of the Scriptures. But on the fifteenth point, the nature of Communion, there was no agreement. Luther refused to budge from the words of Jesus, "This is my body." Zwingli refused to alter his opinion that the bread and wine were symbols of Christ's body and blood. The lack of theological agreement meant there would be no political alliance. Zwingli returned to Zurich without the support of the Protestants in Germany.

Zwingli's example and leadership in Zurich had inspired preachers in other Swiss cities to initiate reform of their churches as well. Zwingli was several times invited to visit and participate in public disputations that usually led to the adoption of reforms. He was in Bern in 1528 and in Basel in 1529. The adoption of reform in Basel in 1529 led the great humanist Erasmus to move away from the city to the traditional catholic city of Freiburg — a city ruled directly by Habsburg relatives of Emperor Charles V.

The more rural Swiss cantons rejected Zwingli's reforms. Five of the cantons actually allied themselves with Archduke Ferdinand (Charles V's younger brother) in an attempt to halt the spread of Protestant reform. Tensions escalated dramatically in 1529, when a Zwinglian preacher was arrested and then executed as a heretic by one of the catholic cantons. Zurich and the other reformed cantons demanded the right of Protestant preachers to enter and preach the gospel in all of the Swiss Confederation cantons. The

Catholic cantons responded by sending an army to attack Zurich. Zwingli joined the city militia as they rushed out to meet the invading army. Outnumbered 3-1, the Zurich militia was defeated. Among the dead were over fifty city councilors and pastors — Zwingli among them. The Catholic cantons had no wish to pursue a lengthy civil war, and withdrew their troops based upon an agreement that each canton would have complete freedom to govern itself in matters of religion. Catholic cantons would stay Catholic and reformed Protestant cantons would be free to continue their reforms.

Zwingli's work firmly established the final authority of Scripture in all matters of theology and church practice in most of the major cities of Switzerland. Under his successors in Zurich and later in Geneva, the Protestant churches prospered.

Zwingli and the militia prepare to meet the armies of the Catholic Cantons.

Chapter 21

Thomas Müntzer 1488-1525

Thomas Müntzer was born in 1488, in the village of Stolberg in the Harz Mountains. He entered the University of Leipzig in 1506, at the age of 18. In 1512, he completed a Master of Arts degree at the University of Frankfurt. He was ordained as a priest, and from 1514-1517 he served as confessor at a nunnery in the town of Frohse. He attended lectures at the University of Wittenberg for a year, 1517-18. He then took a position as confessor in a Bernardine convent where the obligations to hear confessions took little of his time. He was thus able to devote himself to continued studies of the church fathers and the Scriptures.

On Martin Luther's recommendation, Müntzer was appointed town preacher in the prosperous central German town of Zwickau in 1520. In Zwickau, Müntzer began attacking the rich and powerful. He denounced local chapter of the Franciscans for their wealth and opulent lifestyle. He also denounced the local nobility for their exploitation of the peasants. In April of 1521, the town council of Zwickau expelled Müntzer because of his radical views.

Müntzer went to Bohemia (the modern-day Czech Republic) and stayed for some months in Prague. Because of the intense interest in everyone associated with Luther, he was invited to preach in Jan Hus' old church, the Bethlehem Chapel. In November of 1521, he composed a manifesto which was printed and posted on church doors in Prague. In the *Prague Manifesto*, Müntzer denounced the nobility, the clergy, and the learned for their perversion and suppression of the gospel. He called upon the common people to take control of the church, elect their own pastors and proclaim the true gospel. The Manifesto announced that the End of the Age was near and that the elect must gather together and separate from the world.

When the people of Prague failed to respond to the Manifesto, Müntzer left the city and returned to Saxony. In early 1522, he was appointed to preach by the town council of Allstedt, a small town near the northern border of Saxony. He was seen as an ally of Luther and an advocate of his reform program for the church. From 1523 to 1524, he led the reform of worship in Allstedt. He insisted that the Mass be abolished and that the entire liturgy be translated into German so that the common people could understand and participate. So far this much was good, but there were hints that Müntzer had further steps beyond church reform in mind. One of the prayers he instituted in the service was titled, "Deliver us from the anti-christian government of the godless."

Müntzer was confirmed in his hostile view of "godless princes" when the Count of Mansfeld, just across the border from Allstedt, issued a proclamation forbidding his subjects from attending Müntzer's services. Müntzer denounced the Count from the pulpit as, "Godless and heretical ... a miserable and stupid man!"

Müntzer began to quietly recruit a band of followers from among his congregation who served as his bodyguard and private militia. In March of 1524, they attacked a chapel in a neighboring convent and destroyed a statue of the Virgin Mary which the nuns asserted had certain miraculous powers. Müntzer justified this action by pointing to the example of the Old Testament patriarchs' destruction of idols.

In July of 1524, Müntzer was invited to present his views to an audience which included Duke John of Saxony and his son, John Frederick. In his sermon, Müntzer warned the princes that if they did not wield the sword as godly princes, the sword would pass from them to the people. Müntzer was not yet encouraging the people to take up arms against their rulers. However, he clearly warned the rulers that they would face an uprising if they did not ally themselves with the peasants and help them achieve their religious, political, and economic goals.

Within a matter of weeks, the princes responded to Müntzer's sermon by commanding him to dissolve his band of followers and to stop advocating the destruction of chapels or statues. Realizing that the princes might take further action against him, and knowing that the city council would neither support nor protect him, Müntzer fled Allstedt in August of 1524.

Müntzer did not travel far. Just to the west of Allstedt, Müntzer received refuge in the Saxon town of Mühlhausen near the border between Saxony and Hesse. Here he was welcomed by Henry Pfeiffer, the town preacher. Pfeiffer had been reforming the churches in the city for over a year. He was at present in the midst of a dispute with the town council over the rights of the more humble citizens to be represented politically. Müntzer immediately began organizing another band of followers, a secret League of the Elect, who would be prepared to oppose the godless. In his letters, Müntzer began to refer to himself as "Thomas Müntzer with the sword of Gideon," "Servant of God against the godless," and "Destroyer of the godless."

Luther sent a letter to the council at Mühlhausen warning them about Müntzer and denouncing him as "the Satan of Allstedt." Müntzer and Pfeiffer had already organized their followers into a military band. In September, 200 of them had signed an "eternal covenant" pledging to support the two preachers by force if called upon. This was too much for the town council. At the end of the month, after several riots and nights of unrest in the town, they succeeded in forcing Pfeiffer and Müntzer to flee the city. Müntzer traveled south, first to Nuremburg, then to Basel.

By early 1525, Müntzer's and Pfeiffer's followers succeeded in reversing their political fortunes. The two leading councilman were banished from the city and replaced. Word was sent for the two preachers, inviting them to return to Mühlhausen. This they did and immediately resumed preaching and organizing. By April, Müntzer was reported to have an armed force of 1500 men sworn to "defend the gospel and destroy idolatry." In that same month of April, there began to be outbreaks of violence, unrest, and revolt among peasants in widely scattered locations throughout Germany. Müntzer dispatched a letter to his former followers in Allstedt urging them to rise up, seize the sword, hammer on the princely anvils and destroy their castles. "The godless must be destroyed," he warned.

On April 26th, Müntzer and Pfeiffer mustered their troops outside the walls of the town and marched to the neighboring city of Homburg. There they attacked and plundered the monastery. They were joined by armed bands all day. Many of these small gangs carried plunder from the houses of landowners they had attacked. These small groups had risen up against the landowners of the region, ransacking (and often murdering) those whom Müntzer considered to be the "godless." Müntzer tried to turn the small army in the direction of his old enemy, the Count of Mansfeld. Pfeiffer and others insisted that the territory surrounding Mühlhausen should first be cleansed of the "godless" before they ventured further afield.

The uproar caused by Müntzer's "Christian League" of armed peasants had alarmed both the Landgrave of Hesse, and the Elector of Saxony. It took over a week, but they gathered their forces and prepared to confront the peasant band which was assembled at the town of Frankenhausen about halfway between Allstedt and Mühlhausen. On May 14th, The twenty-five year old Landgrave Philipp of Hesse opened a parley with the peasants. He told them that the princes understood that many of the peasants had been misled. If they would surrender Thomas Müntzer for punishment, and if the peasants surrendered, the princes promised to treat them with kindness and charity. After some debate, the peasants rejected Philipp's demands.

Müntzer encouraged his followers, proclaiming that God was at work through them to cleanse the world of the godless. God was on the side of the peasants, he told them. The peasants marched out of the city walls towards the troops, singing a hymn. They believed what Müntzer had told them, that they would be miraculously protected from the bullets of their enemies. When the first volley of musket and cannon fire hit, killing and wounding the peasants, they panicked and ran for cover — towards the trees and the town walls. Before the day was over, at least 5,000 peasants had been killed.

Both Pfeiffer and Müntzer were captured. Thomas Müntzer was found hiding in a bed in the attic of a house just inside the city gate. After being questioned and tortured, Müntzer and Pfeiffer were executed by beheading on May 25th, 1525. The entire revolt in Thuringia had lasted barely three weeks.

Luther was appalled at the bloodshed, but considered that events had clearly demonstrated that Müntzer was a false prophet.

Chapter 22

Conrad Grebel 1498-1526 & Michael Sattler 1490?-1527

The reform movement started by Zwingli in Zurich spread rapidly. Immediately after the Great Disputations of 1524 and the institution of reforms in the churches of Zurich, other reform-minded preachers were at work in the cities along the Rhine. The Rhine, in southern Germany flows from east to west, just north of Zurich, and then turns north at Basel as it heads for the great cities of Strasburg, Heidelberg, Mainz, and Cologne. In St. Gall the university-educated preacher Vadian successfully persuaded the city council to adopt Zwinglian reforms. In Schaffhausen, there was great popular support for reform. In Waldshut, Balthasar Hubmaier led reform. In Basel, Capito and Oecolampadius led reform — assisted by Zwingli. In Strasburg, the former Dominican monk, Martin Bucer reformed the church.

Conrad Grebel was born around 1500. He was the son of one of the Zurich city councilors. He had studied at the University of Basel, then at the University of Vienna, and finally at the University of Paris. He returned from Paris to Zurich in 1520. Zwingli had organized a group that met regularly to study the languages of Greek and Hebrew and to apply their skills to Bible study. Conrad Grebel joined the group. By all accounts he was a gifted student and a devoted supporter of Zwingli's reforms.

But by 1524, especially after the second Great Disputation, Grebel was growing increasingly impatient with Zwingli. He felt that Zwingli was moving too slowly. Grebel complained that Zwingli was not consistently applying the Scriptures. He also felt that

Zwingli had committed a grievous error by allowing the City Council of Zurich (the secular authorities) to take control of the reform of the church. In particular, Grebel had been encouraging Zwingli to deal with the issue of infant baptism. Grebel could find no Scriptural justification for the baptism of infants. Had not Jesus been baptized as an adult? Had John the Baptist baptized any infants? Were not the Ethiopian eunuch and Cornelius the Centurion baptized as adults? Several private meetings were held with Zwingli and his circle of preachers and Bible study students — Grebel had been a part of the circle for four years now — at which the matter of infant baptism was debated. In late 1524, Conrad Grebel's wife gave birth to a daughter. Grebel made a conscious decision not to have the baby baptized. Others who shared Grebel's views began to preach against infant baptism in churches in and around Zurich. The Town Council acted in January 1525, calling for a public disputation on the issue of infant baptism.

At the disputation, Zwingli strongly defended the practice of infant baptism. He asserted that there was nothing in Scripture which forbade the practice. He argued that just as circumcision was the sign of the covenant for infants in the Old Testament, baptism was the sign of the covenant for infants in the New Testament. The Council, after hearing Zwingli's arguments and hearing Grebel's arguments, decided in favor of Zwingli. They ordered Grebel and his friends to cease preaching against infant baptism. Four days later, Grebel and his friends met at the house of a prominent citizen, Felix Mantz. George Blaurock, a preacher, asked Conrad Grebel to baptize him in the name of Jesus Christ. After Grebel complied, at their request, Blaurock baptized the other men present. The Hutterite Chronicle comments, "Therewith was the separation from the world and its evil works begun."

After their rejection by the town council, Grebel and the other Anabaptists left Zurich and began preaching in neighboring Swiss cities. Balthasar Hubmaier, the reformer of the city of Waldshut, welcomed them. In April of 1525, he was publicly re-baptized in the town church. It is important to realize that these developments occurred as Thomas Müntzer was calling on peasants to rise up and kill their godless masters all over Germany. The Peasant's Revolt was a frightening spectacle to the officials of the Swiss towns. Some of the citizens of Waldshut even joined the peasant militia bands in southwest Germany.

By October, Grebel (along with Mantz and Blaurock) had returned to the vicinity of Zurich. They were once again preaching and organizing a gathered church of re-baptized, adult believers in some of the small towns south of the city. The officials in Zurich had all three arrested. Then the Zurich city council called for a second disputation on the issue of infant baptism. Zwingli was intensely annoyed that Grebel and his friends had refused to accept defeat after the first disputation. The disputation was held on November 6-8, 1525. Not surprisingly, the council ruled that Zwingli had prevailed with his arguments defending the legitimacy of infant baptism.

Grebel, Mantz, and Blaurock were sentenced to prison indefinitely "because of their re-baptism and improper practice." Shortly after their trial, however, the three Anabaptist leaders managed to escape from their captivity by climbing through an open window. Their freedom was short-lived. Grebel died of the plague in a small Swiss village the following year. George Blaurock fled south to the Italian/Alpine region called the Tyrol where he organized Anabaptist congregations for three years. Then, in 1528, he was arrested, charged with heresy and treason, and burned at the stake in 1529. Felix Mantz was recaptured by the Zurich authorities in late 1526 and was executed by drowning.

Among Grebel's followers who had been ordered to pay fines and cease their preaching was one Michael Sattler, a former Benedictine monk. We know very little about Michael Sattler's parents, his youth, or his education. When he first appears in the historical record, he is already a Benedictine Monk at a monastery in the Black Forest region of southwestern Germany — not far from Switzerland. He must have been a reasonably promising and intelligent young man, for he had risen to a position as prior (or second in command) of the monastery. During the Peasant Uprisings of 1524-1525, a peasant militia force occupied the monastery, causing the abbot to flee to the nearby city of Freiburg. When the peasants left, Prior Michael Sattler seems to have left the monastery as well. He traveled southwards, with some of the militia men from the city of Waldshut, towards the city of Zurich where Zwingli and his followers were reforming the church. At this stage there is no clear evidence that Sattler's convictions had progressed beyond a rejection of the monastic life and a general openness to the reform of the church along Biblical lines.

In Zurich and Waldshut, Sattler came in contact with the followers of Grebel, Blaurock, and Mantz. He was intrigued by their rejection of infant baptism and advocacy of a "separated church" composed of only those who had, as adults, made a profession of faith and been baptized. By 1526, Sattler had left Zurich and was advocating a "separated church" in the towns of southwest Germany, and for a time in the city of Strasburg.

In February 1527, he left Strasburg and traveled to the little town of Schleitheim on the Swiss-German border, just north of Zurich for a meeting with other Anabaptist leaders. The little group, much diminished because of the persecution in Zurich and elsewhere, drew up a list of seven articles that defined their understanding of what it meant to be a Christian and a part of the Body of Christ. The Schleitheim Confession of Faith consisted of seven points on the following topics:

1. **Baptism** (only for adults who have made a personal profession);

2. **The Ban** (to be used to discipline those who continue in sin);

3. **Communion** (to be reserved for the baptized);

4. **Separation from evil and the world** (including the "devilish weapons of force");

5. **The Duties of Pastors**;

6. **The Sword** (absolutely rejected, because it is "outside the perfection of Christ." No Christian may employ the sword, serve as judge, or accept the office of magistrate);

7. **Oaths** (rejected on the explicit command of Jesus).

Within a month of the Schleitheim Conference, Michael Sattler and his wife were arrested. The accounts of the arrest and trial are the only references we have to her. Arrested with them were a dozen or so other Anabaptists in the little town of Horb on the Neckar river. Unfortunately, Horb was in territory ruled by the Austrian Habsburgs, and they were determined to suppress all heretics, especially the Anabaptists. Sattler and his fellow-prisoners were taken north, down the Neckar river to the town of Rothenberg for trial. After a month's delay, a two-day trial was held. The court found them all guilty of heresy and treason and sentenced them to death.

Accounts seem to indicate that as Sattler answered his accusers, he began to win the sympathy of those attending the trial. The simplicity and the sincerity of his answers pleased them. The judges began to question Sattler about some of his opinions about taking up arms against the Turks. Here is his answer, taken from a transcript of the trial:

> "... if the Turks come, we ought not to resist them. For it is written, Thou shalt not kill. We must not defend ourselves against the Turks and other of our persecutors, but are to beseech God with earnest prayer to repel and resist them ... if warring were right, I would rather take the field against so-called Christians who persecute, capture and kill pious Christians than against the Turks ... The Turk is a true Turk, knows nothing of the Christian faith and is a Turk after the flesh. But you who would be Christians and who make your boast of Christ persecute the pious witnesses of Christ and are Turks after the Spirit!"[26]

This opinion was so shocking that the crowd turned against him. They could not understand why anyone would refuse to defend his countrymen against a foreign invader. The judges too, were angered and alienated. Sattler was found guilty of heresy and condemned. He was burned at the stake in May of 1527. His wife was drowned a few days later.

Chapter 23

Melchior Hoffman, Jan Matthys, & Menno Simons 1496-1561

After the deaths of Grebel, Mantz, and Sattler, many of the other Anabaptist leaders fled Switzerland and Southwestern Germany in search of a place where they could live in peace. As you read in the last chapter, George Blaurock went south into Italy and established Anabaptist congregations in the Tyrol. Balthasar Hubmaier, the reformer of Waldhut who had been baptized by Grebel, headed east, first to Augsburg, and when the authorities reacted unfavorably to his preaching there, he moved on, to Moravia. In Moravia, his preaching attracted some of the nobility, who were converted and baptized by Hubmaier. In a short time, he had established several dozen Anabaptist congregations throughout the region. The rapid growth of the Anabaptists was soon checked, however. Another Anabaptist preacher, Jan Hut, came to Moravia and began teaching that not only should Christians not bear the sword, but they also should not obey it. Hut urged his followers to reject the jurisdiction of the courts and encouraged them to refuse to pay taxes. This was more than the local nobility could tolerate. In a short time, the rejection of infant baptism was made illegal and the Anabaptist leaders were arrested and many were executed. Hubmaier had to flee for his life, but, unfortunately went further east into the heart of Habsburg Catholic territory. In 1528, he was recognized in Vienna, arrested, tried, and burned at the stake. His wife, just as firm in her convictions as her husband was drowned. Jan Hut was arrested in Augsburg and died in prison.

The Moravian Brethren survived, but only barely. They were joined by many of the followers of George Blaurock from the Tyrol in northern Italy, most notably by his successor as leader, Jacob Huter. Huter and his followers believed in the common ownership of goods among all believers and he rapidly organized the Moravian Brethren into small communal farming communities. Although Huter himself was arrested and executed in 1536, the Moravian Brethren (or Hutterites as they came to be called) survived centuries of persecution and continue to exist as small communities of believers — including several farming communes in South Dakota in the United States.

While Hubmaier, Blaurock, Hut, and Huter were spreading the Anabaptist message down the Danube valley to the east, other Swiss Brethren were moving northwards down the Rhine. For a time, there was a substantial Brethren, or Anabaptist, community in Strasburg. Martin Bucer, the reformer of Strasburg, persuaded the city council not to persecute the Anabaptists. He hoped instead that they could be persuaded to drop their objections to infant baptism through dialogue and discussion.

Unfortunately, the Anabaptist congregation in Strasburg gave rise to a fanatical and extravagant preacher whose memory was to be an embarrassment to Anabaptists for centuries. His name was Melchior Hoffman. He was not a learned man, but had completed an apprenticeship and become a journeyman furrier. He had been attracted early to the cause of reforming the church and visited both Zwingli in Zurich and Luther in Wittenberg. After that, he spent time as an itinerant preacher in Northern Germany and Scandinavia.

In 1529, he joined the Anabaptists in Strasburg. In his preaching, he spoke increasingly of the Second Coming, which he predicted would occur very shortly. He told his audiences that only the Brethren, who had been baptized as adults, would rule with Christ. The city officials in Strasburg quickly expelled Hoffman and barred him from the city. Hoffman traveled northwards, down the Rhine and found a more receptive audience in the low countries. In the space of just a few years, large groups of believers, calling themselves Melchiorites, were established. Hoffman began claiming to be the prophet Elijah and predicted that there would shortly be a day of wrath in which all but the righteous would perish. In 1533, Hoffman returned to Strasburg, was quickly recognized, arrested, and imprisoned. Even now, Bucer could not bring himself to advocate the execution of an Anabaptist leader, even one as extreme as Hoffman. He continued to hope that Hoffman might be persuaded to renounce his more outlandish opinions and embrace the orthodox faith. Hoffman spent ten years in prison in Strasburg and appears never to have wavered in his opinions.

His followers in the Netherlands continued to meet secretly and expectantly — looking for the imminent Second Coming of Christ. From among these followers, there now arose an even more dangerous leader. His name was Jan Matthys, a baker from the Dutch city of Haarlem. Matthys began to tell his audiences that, in order for Christ to return, the righteous must seize power from the unrighteous. Matthys traveled from city to city, baptizing and organizing small armed bands who would rise up when he gave the signal.

In 1534, Matthys received the opportunity to put his plans in to action. The German city of Münster had declared itself Lutheran in 1532, expelling the Catholic Bishop who had held both secular and spiritual power there. In January of 1534, the two Lutheran preachers who had been most active in reforming churches in the city were persuaded by the Anabaptists to renounce infant baptism. Matthys and the other Melchiorites saw this as a sign of the imminent return of Christ. Münster, as the first city to embrace true Anabaptist doctrine, was hailed as the new Jerusalem. Matthys came personally to Münster and assumed control. His first actions were to cleanse the city of the unrighteous. Those who would not make personal professions of faith and be baptized as adults were driven from the city. Matthys further proclaimed the communal ownership of all property in the city and ordered all books except the Bible destroyed. Those who objected were executed, with Matthys himself striking some of the blows. When the Bishop of Münster appeared before the city with an army and began a siege, Matthys assumed command of the military defense of the city as well. Shortly after the arrival of the Bishop's army, Matthys proclaimed that he had had a vision. He said God had promised him that, like Gideon, he would vanquish their foes with a small band of picked men from among the righteous. When Matthys led his small party out to attack the besieging army, he was promptly killed.

The leadership of the Anabaptists in the city now passed to one of Matthys' young disciples, Jan Bockelson, also known as Jan of Leiden. In addition to communal ownership of property, Jan declared that God had commanded the saints to revive the practice of polygamy. He himself proceeded to marry fifteen wives. When an assault by the besieging army in the summer of 1534 failed, Jan proclaimed it to be a sign that the righteous of Münster would soon inherit the earth. He had himself crowned King. But Münster was still cut off. The soldiers of the Catholic bishop were soon joined by reinforcements sent by the Lutheran Landgraf of Hesse. The population of the city were in desperate straits, many starving to death while King Jan held lavish banquets at his court. Finally in 1535, the besieging soldiers succeeded in breaking through the city walls. The Anabaptists of Münster were all executed. King Jan and some of his aides were captured, tortured to death and their bodies placed in iron cages hung from the bell tower of the church.

The year long spectacle of the wild-eyed, millenarians at Münster haunted the Anabaptists for centuries thereafter. Their opponents used the behavior there as evidence that the Anabaptists were unbalanced, and dangerous anarchists. Because the leaders of Münster had rejected infant baptism, all such teaching was associated with rejection of all civil authority. Anabaptists everywhere were denounced and persecuted as revolutionaries.

The shocking events at Münster had a profound impact on one future leader of the Anabaptists, Menno Simons. At the time of the Münster uprising, Simons was a catholic priest in a small Dutch town. One of his brothers became an Anabaptist and joined the throng at Münster. When Münster fell, Menno Simons' brother was executed.

Menno had already become convinced that Luther and Zwingli's criticisms of the catholic church were justified. He believed, with them, that the only authority for Christians and for the church should be the Bible. He was appalled at the excesses committed by Matthys and Jan of Leiden at Münster and resolved to spend his life in preaching and teaching Biblical truth. Like the other Anabaptists, he rejected infant baptism. Unlike the Melchiorites, he turned away from millennial proclamations and rejected the use of force. Simons returned to the principles of Conrad Grebel and Michael Sattler, and the other points contained in the Schleitheim Confession.

In 1539, Simons published a systematic summary of Anabaptist theology called *The Book of Fundamentals*. It was a more thorough, systematic treatment of the Anabaptist principles first identified by Grebel and Sattler. The book was very influential, emphasizing a strong commitment to Biblical authority, and salvation by faith through grace. Simons was also firm and articulate in his rejection of the use of force. *The Book of Fundamentals* became a guide for Anabaptist preachers and congregations for many years.

By 1542, with a wife and three children, Menno Simons was traveling in disguise, hiding and preaching after dark to small congregations in the towns of the Netherlands. When the bishop of Cologne flirted, for a time, with Lutheranism and religious toleration, Simons moved there. By 1545, he was then back in the Netherlands in the area around Emden.

The Netherlands were ruled by a succession of Habsburg governors who were determined to root out all heresy — whether Lutheran or Anabaptist. Although the Anabaptists continued to suffer persecution — banishment, arrest, and execution — Menno Simons was fiercely protected and always warned before he could be arrested. Although forced to spend almost all his life in hiding, Menno Simons did remain free. He guided and directed the Anabaptist community for over twenty-five years, until his death in 1561. Those who followed his teaching came to be known as Mennonites, a name they continue to bear today.

Chapter 24

Henry VIII 1491-1547

When young prince Henry was born in 1491, his father Henry Tudor had been king of England for six years and his elder brother was five years old. As the second son of the king, he was prepared for a career in the church, not expecting to ever be king himself.

Young Prince Henry's education was fashioned after the model of the renaissance prince. He was a good student and easily mastered classical Latin, reading extensively in the classics of Roman literature as well as works of theology. But Henry was not a bookworm. He also excelled in the martial arts, in riding, and in hunting. In 1501, Henry's elder brother Arthur (15) married Catherine of Aragon (16), one of the daughters of Ferdinand and Isabella of Spain. Four and a half months later, Arthur died, leaving his young bride a widow and his younger brother as the new heir to the throne. Henry's future prospects now shifted. Rather than becoming a bishop, he would become king. Within the year, Henry VII arranged for Catherine's betrothal to Prince Henry, even though he was only twelve at the time.

In April of 1509, Henry VII died and eighteen year old Henry VIII was crowned as his successor. In June, he married the twenty-four year old Catherine of Aragon. Catherine's nephew, Charles (future King of Spain and Holy Roman Emperor) was nine years old.

Over the next six years, Catherine and Henry had six children — only one of whom survived.27 Two daughters were stillborn, two sons were stillborn, and one son lived for six weeks. Only the Princess Mary, born in 1516 was alive by the year 1526. Catherine had had no other children in eight years.

The tragedy of the deaths of five children seems to have had a deep effect on Henry. He became convinced that God was punishing him — and that the reason for that punishment was his marriage to his brother's wife. It was vitally important to Henry that he have a male heir to succeed to the throne. God's curse upon his children could only mean that his marriage had offended God. The solution, to Henry, was clear. He must be allowed to renounce his marriage to Catherine and take a different wife.

The man King Henry charged with accomplishing this task was his chief minister, Lord Chancellor, Cardinal Wolsey. Wolsey (1471-1530), had been born the son of a small butcher in Suffolk. He attended Oxford University where he proved an able student. He moved steadily upward in church circles and in 1515 he came to the attention of the young King Henry VIII. Henry liked the older Wolsey's ideas, especially his strong case for strengthening the alliance with Spain and attempting to recover the territory England had lost to France. He named Wolsey to the post of his chief minister, the king's Lord Chancellor. When the Archbishopric of York became vacant, Henry secured it for Wolsey. In 1518, Pope Leo X (persuaded, it was said by a large quantity of English money) appointed Wolsey to the College of Cardinals. He also named Wolsey as the Papal Legate — the Pope's official representative in England. From 1518 on, Wolsey was the head of the church in England.

In 1526, then, Wolsey was in perfect position to see to it that Henry's request for an annulment of his marriage was granted — so Henry thought. For Wolsey, the matter was more complicated. An annulment of the king's marriage could only be granted by the Pope. Unfortunately a papal dispensation had been granted to allow the marriage in 1509. Now Pope Clement VII was being asked to reverse the dispensation granted 17 years earlier by Pope Julius II. Pope Clement was not immediately persuaded. Wolsey persisted, and informed the king that it was only a matter of time and the skillful use of his influence. But before Wolsey had time to finish his diplomatic work, the troops of the Holy Roman Emperor, Charles V, seized the city of Rome. The Pope became the virtual prisoner of the Emperor. Since Catherine was Charles V's aunt, the Pope was reluctant to annul her eighteen year marriage. Henry was furious.

Wolsey had failed. In 1529, Henry dismissed him from office and shortly thereafter had him arrested. Since the Pope had refused his direct request, Henry had his marriage secretly annulled by a church court in England. In Wolsey's place, Henry appointed Sir Thomas More as his chief minister and Lord Chancellor.

Henry's quarrel with the Pope did not make him a Protestant. In fact, he was an outspoken opponent of Luther and his followers and encouraged the bishops in their suppression of heretical opinions. In 1521, Henry read of Luther's attack on the seven sacraments (Luther believed that only two — Baptism and Communion were taught in the New Testament). Henry took it upon himself to write a treatise called *The Defense of the Seven Sacraments*. He dedicated it to Pope Leo X. Duly flattered, The Pope, conferred upon Henry the title "Defender of the Faith."

Henry was not satisfied with the secret annulment. He desperately wanted the annulment of his marriage recognized by the church. Since requests and diplomacy had failed, he turned to threats and blackmail to accomplish his goal. In 1529, he summoned both Parliament and a Convocation of the Clergy. In Parliament, his ministers introduced legislation reducing the fees and incomes of the clergy. In Convocation, the bishops were forced to pass a bill acknowledging Henry as the head of the church in England, "so far as the law of Christ allows."

Pope Clement remained more impressed by the presence of Charles V's troops in Rome than he was by the threats of legislation in the English Parliament. He continued to turn a deaf ear to Henry's requests. After two years of delay, in 1532, the English bishops adopted a bill called *The Submission of the Clergy*. Thomas Cranmer was confirmed as the new Archbishop of Canterbury, and Sir Thomas More resigned as Lord Chancellor.

In January of 1533, Henry secretly married Anne Boleyn. In March, Parliament passed a statute forbidding appeals from decisions by the church in England to any other sovereign. Archbishop Cranmer announced his decision that Henry's marriage to Catherine was invalid. Princess Elizabeth was born in September of 1533 to Queen Anne Boleyn.

In 1534, Parliament passed the *Act of Supremacy* which had several effects. First, it declared the King of England to be the Supreme Head of the English church instead of the Pope. Secondly, it made clear who was in the line of succession and who was not. As the child of an annulled marriage, princess Mary was disinherited. Elizabeth's claim to the throne (and the claim of any other children which Queen Anne Boleyn might have) was made primary. Further, the Act required all subjects to swear an oath recognizing the children of King Henry and Queen Anne as his only legitimate heirs. Only Bishop John Fisher and Sir Thomas More refused to take the oath. Both were executed in 1535.

In January of 1536, Queen Anne gave birth to a stillborn son. Catherine of Aragon died the same month. In May of 1536, Anne Boleyn was imprisoned in the tower, charged with adultery, and executed two weeks later. Historians still disagree about whether the charges against her may or may not have been true. What is clear is that a group of noblemen and bishops (many of them still loyal to the Roman Catholic church and opposed to Henry's break with Rome) persuaded the King that Queen Anne Boleyn had betrayed him. The accusers of Queen Anne were joined at a critical moment by the King's chief minister, Thomas Cromwell.

On May 30th, less than a week after the execution of Anne Boleyn, Henry married Jane Seymour. Jane had been at court for several years and had served as a maid to Catherine of Aragon. She used her influence to bring about a reconciliation between Henry and his daughter Mary. Seventeen months after her marriage to Henry, Jane gave birth to Prince Edward in October of 1537 and died 12 days later. Henry was crushed.

The successors to Wolsey and More, principal secretary Cromwell and Archbishop Cranmer, strongly supported Henry in his break with Rome (you will read more about them in a later chapter). They wanted him to move further in the direction of reform. It is not clear that the king was altogether enthusiastic about their plans, but the advantages to the crown of what they proposed appealed to him. Beginning in 1536, Cromwell shepherded legislation through Parliament which dissolved all English monasteries and confiscated their land and possessions for the crown. In the beginning, only the smaller monasteries were seized (on the grounds that they were corrupt and lax in their morals), but by 1540 all the monasteries had been dissolved.

In January of 1540, Henry married for the fourth time, to Anne of Cleves. The marriage had been arranged by Cromwell who hoped to secure an alliance between England and the German Protestant princes. He had been assured that Anne was a beautiful and attractive lady who would charm the king. He went so far as to commission a portrait of Anne which he presented to the king. But Cromwell and the King were both deceived. When Anne arrived in England, Henry was appalled to discover that she was older than he had expected, plain in looks (downright ugly, according to some), and she spoke little English. Nevertheless, the treaty and marriage arrangements which Cromwell had negotiated were carried out. Although Henry slept at Anne's side, the marriage was never consummated and the couple are said to have spent the night hours playing cards together. Anne was soon sent to Richmond Palace, ostensibly for her health, open air and pleasure. She raised no objection to divorce proceedings when Henry began them. The marriage was declared null and void on 9 July 1540, just six months after the service. Cromwell was sent to the tower and beheaded on July 28th, 1540. By all accounts, Henry and Anne remained good friends after the divorce.

On the day of Cromwell's death, Henry VIII married Catherine Howard, the daughter of a conservative Catholic family. This fifth marriage proved a disaster. Catherine Howard was a spoiled, silly courtier, and she showed an appalling lack of sense and self-control. The court was soon swirling with rumors of her infidelity to the King. There are no doubts that the charges were true. Once the rumors became public knowledge, Archbishop Cranmer had the unenviable task of breaking the news to King Henry. After an investigation in which she admitted the truth of the charges, Catherine was beheaded for adultery in February of 1542. She and Henry had been married for less than 20 months.

About 18 months later, in July of 1543, Henry married thirty-one year old Catherine Parr. Catherine kept Henry company, nursed him, read to him, debated with him, and ultimately, outlived him. She had been twice married and twice widowed before she married Henry. Henry was fifty, and in failing health. His relationship with Catherine was a warm one and their marriage lasted until his death in January of 1547. After Henry died she remarried again, to Thomas Seymour, the brother of Jane Seymour, Henry's third wife. She gave birth to a daughter in August of 1548, but both she and the child died within a week.

Henry never considered himself a Protestant. Though he broke with Rome and refused to recognize the authority of the Pope, he continued to support many of the doctrines of the Roman Catholic church. Indeed, in 1539, he introduced to Parliament a summary of religious practices to be enforced in England called the Six Articles. The draft of the bill has revisions in Henry's own hand and he appeared in the House of Lords personally during the debate to argue for its passage. The Six Articles affirmed transubstantiation, communion in one kind, clerical celibacy, the validity of vows of celibacy, private masses, and auricular confession. Anyone denying any of the articles was subject to being burned as a heretic and suffering the loss of all their property. Two days after the execution of Cromwell in 1540, three Catholics were executed on charges of treason, and three Protestants were burned as heretics.

Henry died on January 27th, 1547, at the age of 55, attended by Archbishop Cranmer who had enjoyed the king's trust until the end. In his will he left large endowments so that many masses might be said for the repose of his soul.

Henry left three surviving children by three different wives: the Princess Mary by Catherine of Aragon, the Princess Elizabeth by Anne Boleyn, and Prince Edward by Jane Seymour. Both Edward and Elizabeth had been raised in their father's household and educated by tutors with strong Protestant convictions. Mary had been raised in her mother's household as a strong Catholic. For obvious reasons, she disapproved of her father's religious policies on almost every count. In his will, Henry specified that the crown would pass first to Prince Edward, and then, if he had no heir, to Princess Mary, and finally, if she had no heir, to Princess Elizabeth. The terms of Henry's will (with the short exception of the nine day reign of Queen Jane) were followed exactly. Edward reigned from 1547-1553, Mary from 1553 to 1558, and Elizabeth from 1558-1603.

Chapter 25

Thomas More 1477-1535

Thomas More was born in London in 1477. As a young boy, he studied at St. Anthony's School, one of the prestigious, private cathedral schools which trained youths who showed great academic promise. When Thomas was eight years old, there was a political revolution in England. The long war between the houses of Lancaster and York ended in the climactic battle of Bosworth Field. King Richard III was killed on the battlefield and the crown was claimed by young Henry Tudor, who was crowned as King Henry VII. It was the last battle in the War of the Roses which had pitted the noble families of Lancaster and York against each other for more than thirty years. More, a boy of 8, remembered for the rest of his life, the rejoicing in his household when they heard the news, for King Richard was widely known to be a scoundrel and was an unpopular king.

When More was a few years older, he served in the household of the Archbishop of Canterbury, Cardinal Morton. From the Archbishop's household, More went on to attend Oxford University where he studied Greek under Thomas Linacre (who had learned his Greek from the Medici's Platonic Academy in Florence).

The goal of Thomas More's education was to prepare him for a career as a lawyer. His parents hoped that his intellectual skills would lead to a successful career as a lawyer, and perhaps a lucrative appointment as a minor royal official. While he was in London, studying the law, Thomas More attended a series of lectures given by William Grocyn on

St. Augustine's book, *The City of God*. The lectures affected him deeply. He reflected on his own life and compared it with St. Augustine's. He wanted his life to count for something. He wanted to be able to serve God in the way in which Augustine had. For a brief time, he considered renouncing the world and becoming a monk.

While he considered the possibility of taking vows, his legal career began to prosper. In 1502, at the age of twenty-five, he was appointed under-sheriff of London. The office was the equivalent to our modern day district attorney. His main duties were to represent the city in all of its legal actions in various courts. His skill at the law, and his eloquent representation of his clients soon brought him to the attention of the Lord Chancellor, and King Henry VII, himself.

In 1505, at age twenty-eight, More married Jane Colt. With her he would have three daughters. Four years after their marriage, King Henry VII died, and his son, Prince "Hal" was crowned as King Henry VIII. Well-educated, possessing a firm grounding in the classics, and demonstrating a mastery of classical Latin, the young Henry VIII was considered to be the epitome of the Renaissance Prince. More was honored to be chosen to serve the young, cultured king -- and would have proudly served him in any capacity.

In 1521, King Henry appointed More Treasurer of the Exchequer. In 1523 he was elected Speaker of the House of Commons. In 1529, More succeeded Cardinal Wolsey as Lord Chancellor of England — the king's chief minister. It was as Henry VIII's chief minister that More and the King came into conflict.

King Henry VIII's marriage to Catherine of Aragon had produced no male heir. Though Henry and Catherine had a daughter, the King desperately wanted a son — for many reasons, but chiefly to ensure that when he died, the crown would pass peacefully to his successor. In all of her history, England had never been ruled by a Queen and Henry questioned whether or not the people would accept a ruling Queen.

Henry had gradually become convinced that his lack of a son was a result of God's judgment. Catherine of Aragon, his wife, had previously been married to Henry's elder brother Arthur, who had died. Henry succeeded his father as king rather than his brother and had married his brother's widow. Now he came to the conclusion that the marriage had been a mistake. He believed that God would never bless him with a son, because he had done something forbidden in scripture, he had married his brother's widow. Henry prepared a formal request to the Pope asking the Pope to annul his marriage on the grounds that it had been against God's law from the start. When the Pope refused to grant the annulment, Henry made plans to proclaim himself the head of the church in England so that he could have the English church annul his marriage.

Thomas More, as Henry's Lord Chancellor, and a devout son of the Roman church was caught between two loyalties. He wished to serve and obey his King, but he also wished to remain loyal to the church and the Pope. In 1532, when King Henry VIII made the break with Rome official, Thomas More resigned as Lord Chancellor. In 1533, King Henry married Anne Boleyn, his second wife.

In 1534, Parliament passed the Act of Succession in which the children of Henry VIII and Anne Boleyn were recognized as his only legitimate successors. All subjects were required to swear an oath in support of the Act. Thomas More was one of the few who refused to take the oath.

The only Bishop to refuse the oath, John Fisher, was beheaded on June 22nd, 1535. Shortly thereafter, More was put on trial, charged with treason. More steadfastly maintained that although he would not take the oath, he had never uttered a word of treason against his king. At his trial, one of his clerks testified, apparently quite falsely, that he had heard More denying the authority of the King and the legitimacy of his marriage to Anne Boleyn.

More leaped to his feet and cried out, "In Faith, Mr. Rich, I am sorrier for your perjury than for my own peril ..."[28]

The court condemned More for treason, and on July 6th, 1535, he was taken from the tower and beheaded. When the Emperor, Charles V, heard of More's execution, he told the English ambassador,

> "... if we had been master of such a servant, we would rather have lost the best city of our dominions, than have lost such a worthy councilor."[29]

Though, as we will see in the next chapter, Thomas More was certainly no friend of those who were trying to reform the church, he is remembered for his courage in refusing to compromise his convictions -- even though it cost him his life.

Chapter 26

William Tyndale 1494-1536

Williiam Tyndale was born in Gloucestershire, near the border with Wales sometime around 1494. He entered Magdalen School at Oxford at about the age of twelve in 1506. He received a BA degree in 1512 and an MA degree three years later, both from Magdalen Hall, Oxford.

By 1500 Oxford was beginning to be known internationally as a center of the study of Greek. William Grocyn, Thomas Linacre, and William Latimer, all notable Oxford scholars, had studied at the Platonic Academy in Florence. They brought Greek manuscripts, dictionaries and grammar books with them when they returned from Italy. Tyndale learned his Greek from men who had mastered the language in Italy.

After completing his studies at Oxford, Tyndale spent a short time at Cambridge before returning home to Gloucestershire. On his return home, he took a position as tutor for the sons of one of the local minor noblemen. In addition to his teaching duties, Tyndale preached (he had been ordained as a priest) and worked on translation projects. In a short time, he began to receive a reputation as quite a gifted preacher.

While serving as tutor in Gloucestershire, he also found time to translate a little book by Erasmus, the *Enchiridion militis Christiani*, or the *Manual of the Christian Knight*, from Latin into English. Erasmus already enjoyed a reputation as a leading scholar and critic of the church. He was also widely admired not only as a scholar, but as someone who wanted to live the simple Christian life. In the *Enchiridion*, Erasmus asserts that the Christian Knight's two chief weapons are prayer and knowledge of the Scriptures.

In addition to reading Erasmus in the early 1520's, Tyndale was almost certainly reading Martin Luther's criticisms of the Roman church. Luther's views seem to have influenced Tyndale's preaching in the countryside and led to controversy with the local clergy. Tyndale was accused of heresy. Tyndale defended his preaching as being based wholly upon what was plainly taught in Scripture. The charges against him were dismissed, though the church authorities were none too happy with the young man.

Tyndale's experience with the clergy in Gloucestshire convinced him that one of the most serious problems of the church was the lack of knowledge of the Bible. Very few of the parish priests he met knew any Scripture. Hoping to remedy this situation, Tyndale resolved to devote himself to the translation of the Bible into English. In the course of a discussion with a university acquaintance, he said "if God spare my life ere many years, I will cause a boy that driveth the plough, shall know more of the scripture than thou dost."[30]

Tyndale went first to Bishop Tunstall of London in 1523, and asked him to sponsor his translation work. Tunstall had been a student at Oxford in an earlier generation, along with Sir Thomas More. He had studied in Italy and was one of the few English scholars of his day who had mastered Greek. Before becoming Bishop, he had helped Erasmus with the second edition of his Greek New Testament. Tyndale prepared a translation from Greek into English of an essay by the Greek orator Isocrates as a demonstration of his abilities. Tunstall declined the request to become Tyndale's sponsor in the translation project. He did not oppose the project, but he indicated that there was no room on his own staff for Tyndale while he worked.

Tyndale went from the bishop's house disappointed. He was still firm in his resolve to devote himself to translating the Bible into English, but he lacked the means to support himself while he worked on the project. He continued to preach on various occasions, as he was invited, in several churches and chapels in London. The invitations came no doubt through a network of friends, family, and the recommendations of the Walsh family in Gloucestershire for whom he had been a tutor. A wealthy merchant named Henry Monmouth heard one of his sermons and was impressed with the young scholar's intelligence and passion. When he learned that Tyndale had no regular employment, he offered to take him into his own household and support him while he continued his studies and writing. For six months, Tyndale lived with Monmouth and worked on his translation of the Bible.

In the spring of 1524, Tyndale left London for Germany. He next appears in the summer of 1525, in Cologne, printing his own, completed English translation of the New Testament in Cologne. In the intervening year, he may have spent some time in Wittenberg (as some of his enemies charged), though there is no hard evidence to confirm it. In any event, before he could finish printing his book, a Catholic opponent of Luther (who was having a book printed at the same printer) discovered what Tyndale was doing. Tyndale was denounced to the authorities as a heretic — for producing a "Lutheran New Testament, translated into the English language." Tyndale and his assistant fled Cologne one step ahead of his pursuers. They managed to take the printed, but unbound sheets of their book with them.

They headed south, up the Rhine, to the city of Worms and continued their work. By January of 1526 the books were finished. They were seven hundred pages long and about the size of a modern hymn book. Arrangements were quickly made to ship the 3,000 finished copies of the New Testament in English to England. Their arrival in England quickly created an uproar. But nothing in the book identified either its printer or its translator. For many reasons, Tyndale had chosen to publish anonymously.

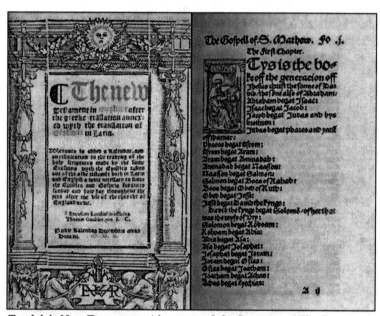

Tyndale's New Testament, *title page and the first page of The Gospel of Saint Matthew*

In England, the appearance of an unauthorized edition of the New Testament in English alarmed the Bishops. At a meeting in the summer of 1526, they resolved that this "untrue translation" should be seized and burned. Any who were found with it should be punished as well. In the fall, Bishop Tunstall of London (who had originally been approached by Tyndale and asked for his support of the translation project) preached a sermon harshly condemning the translation. He claimed he had found over 2,000 errors in it.

In reality, Tyndale's translation was a triumph. Tyndale's skill with both Greek and English were evident throughout. His English reads smoothly and his careful choice of words, tense, and syntax was faithful to the original Greek text. Tyndale's choice of word and phrase were masterful. So much so that 100 years later, when the committee of scholars commissioned by King James worked on their translation, they incorporated Tyndale's work with very few changes. Nine-tenths of the King James Version of the New Testament is Tyndale's.

From 1526-1530, the bishops engaged in a frantic search to find and destroy copies of Tyndale's New Testament and to severely punish (usually by flogging) those who purchased it. Sir Thomas More, soon to be the King's Lord Chancellor, joined in and assisted in the effort to discover and root out heresy. But the stream of books coming into England from the continent continued to grow and could not be stopped. In the summer of 1529, More published a book titled *Dialogue Concerning Heresies,* an attack primarily on Luther and Tyndale. More's attack was couched in strong language and blamed Luther for the peasant's revolt and for the sack of Rome by German troops in 1527. He condemned Tyndale's New Testament as full of errors and heretical. As examples, he cites Tyndale's translation of four key New Testament words (*presbuteros, ekklesia, agape, metanoeo*). For *presbuteros,* Tyndale used "senior"; for *ekklesia,* "congregation"; for *agape,* "love"; and for *metanoeo,* "repent." More insisted they should properly be translated "priest, church, charity, and 'do penance'." It is clear that the supporters of the Roman Catholic church considered Tyndale and his English Bible a great threat. After More became Lord Chancellor, Tyndale replied to his attack and defended his translation. More composed an even longer, more violent attack on Tyndale, which was published in 1532. Tyndale ignored it.

In 1530, religious tensions in England escalated. In January, a priest named Thomas Hitton was arrested in Kent and charged with having preached heretical doctrines. At his trial, he confessed proudly that he had helped to smuggle in copies of the New Testament from abroad. In February, he was found guilty and sentenced to be burned at the stake. His was the first execution of an English Protestant. Tyndale and his friends, now in Antwerp, were shocked and dismayed. The burning of books had been serious, but books could be printed faster than they could be burned. But the prospect of death for the simple possession of an English New Testament was alarming. Tunstall's successor as bishop of London, Stokesly, had little patience with heretics. Where Tunstall had burned books, Stokesly began to burn heretics.

Tyndale found the burning of his New Testament shocking. It embittered him against the bishops in England and against the Roman Catholic church. Henceforth, his editions of the Bible began to include marginal notes which attacked the priesthood, the bishops, the mass and other doctrines of the church quite pointedly.

With the New Testament complete, Tyndale began to translate the books of the Old

Testament. In 1530 his translation of the Pentateuch, the first five books of Moses, appeared in England. In this translation, Tyndale showed himself to be as much a master of Hebrew and its translation into English as he was of Greek. We do not know where Tyndale learned his Hebrew, but it was almost certainly somewhere in Germany. Tyndale was also at work revising his English New Testament. A second, more polished edition was published in 1534. This new edition included a prologue to each book of the New Testament. The prologues (each about a page) are translations (with only a few minor changes) of Luther's prologues from an edition of his German New Testament, which had recently been published in Wittenberg. The longest prologue, for the book of Romans, was thirty-six pages.

In Antwerp, Tyndale lived with the English cloth merchants while continuing his work on the Old Testament. While there, he completed his translations of the historical books of the Old Testament (Joshua, Judges, Ruth, Samuel, Kings, Chronicles, Nehemiah, and Ezra), and started on the Hebrew prophets.

While living in the English Merchant's house, Tyndale enjoyed something like diplomatic immunity. As long as he stayed within the house, local authorities could not arrest him. In 1535, he was befriended by a young Englishman, Henry Phillips, who suddenly appeared on the scene and professed to be an admirer of his translation work. Phillips was in fact a secret agent, probably employed by the Bishop of London, Stokesly. He had been sent to arrange for Tyndale's arrest and execution. On May 21st, Phillips lured Tyndale into town, where he pointed him out to armed officials who were standing by, by prearrangement. Tyndale was seized and taken to prison in a nearby castle. Tyndale's friends made immediate appeals to King Henry VIII and to his chief advisor, Sir Thomas Cromwell who had succeeded Sir Thomas More. Indeed, in one of history's ironies, More was already in prison when Tyndale was arrested, charged with treason against Henry VIII for refusing to take the oath specified in the Act of Supremacy, recognizing the King's marriage to Anne Boleyn. More was executed in July of 1535.

Tyndale's friends hoped that King Henry, now having broken with Rome and showing more sympathy towards the Protestant cause, might use his influence to secure Tyndale's release and allow him to return to England. There were some half-hearted letters of protest written to the authorities in Antwerp, but no serious attempt seems to have been made to secure Tyndale's release.

Tyndale spent more than a year in prison. John Foxe, in his *Book of Martyrs*, records that during this time, Tyndale converted his jailer, his jailer's daughter, and other members of his household. We have one letter he wrote, during that time. It was addressed to the magistrate of the region and asked that he be allowed to have his Hebrew Bible, Hebrew grammar and Hebrew dictionary in his cell so that he might continue his studies. After more than a year in prison, Tyndale was condemned as a heretic and sentenced to be executed. He was strangled and burned at the stake in October of 1536. His last words were "Lord, open the King of England's eyes."

In 1535, the first complete Bible in English had been published by Miles Coverdale in Zurich. After Tyndale's death, in 1537, a second complete Bible in English was published in Antwerp. The title page credits the translation to Thomas Matthew, Esquire. But "Thomas Matthew" was a pseudonym for one John Rogers, chaplain to the English House in Antwerp — a man who had worked closely with Tyndale. The "Matthew Bible" is largely the work of Tyndale. The Pentateuch is Tyndale's. The New Testament is Tyndale's. The books of Job, Psalms, Proverbs, and the Prophets are Coverdale's version, without change. But the rest of the historical books — Joshua, Judges, Ruth, Samuel, Kings, and Chronicles — are almost certainly the last, unpublished translation work of William Tyndale. This new Bible was dedicated to Henry VIII. When the King, at Cromwell and Cranmer's urging authorized its sale in England, it seemed that William Tyndale's final prayer had been answered.

When King James authorized a new translation of the Bible into English in the early 1600's, his committee of scholars took great pains to work from the Greek and Hebrew texts. In the end, though, they found little to improve on from Tyndale's work and kept most of his renderings. Ninety percent of the King James version of the New Testament and fifty percent of the Old Testament can be directly traced to the work done by William Tyndale.

Chapter 27

Thomas Cromwell 1485-1540 &
Thomas Cranmer 1489-1556

T homas Cromwell was born in 1485 in Putney, from a modest background. His father worked variously as a brewer and a blacksmith. Thomas began his rise to fame and power as a mercenary soldier. He then worked for a time for one of the Italian banking houses. Along the way, he learned to read Latin and Italian. Back in England, around 1510, at the age of 25, he took up the study of law, and soon counted among his clients, Cardinal Wolsey. By 1525, he was employed full-time by the Cardinal.

When Wolsey fell from Henry's favor in 1529, Cromwell proved himself to be a nimble politician in a moment of great danger. By 1531, he was a member of the King's council and, having won King Henry's trust, he became the king's principal secretary in 1534. From this position, Cromwell was arguably the 2nd-most powerful person in England, second only to Henry himself. It was from this position that he drafted and had Parliament enact the statutes which dissolved the monasteries in England. His motivation for doing this was only partly to enrich the crown. He also seems to have been genuinely sympathetic with Luther's reforms on the continent. In 1535, he assisted Cranmer (and Queen Anne Boleyn) in securing Henry's permission to have an English Bible placed in every parish church in England, "for every man who will to look and read thereon."

Cromwell made two fatal mistakes in 1540. He arranged Henry's fourth marriage to a German princess whom he had not seen. And he attempted to engage Henry in an alliance with the Lutheran princes of Germany. Henry wanted nothing to do with such an alliance. Henry was deathly afraid that the King of France and the Emperor would form an alliance against him and he always wanted at least one of those two as his own ally. An alliance with the Protestant princes threatened to alienate both of them. Once Henry saw Ann of Cleves, he wanted nothing to do with the marriage either. Cromwell's enemies quickly took advantage of his mistakes. The more conservative bishops (who were still inclined towards a reconciliation with Rome) and some of the nobility whispered in Henry's ear that Cromwell was personally corrupt and perhaps a heretic. Henry was in poor health, in pain, and irritable. He listened to the whisperers and dismissed his minister. Cromwell's enemies had a bill condemning him as a traitor (called a bill of attainder) passed by Parliament and the king signed his execution order. He was beheaded in July of 1540.

Thomas Cranmer was born in 1489, to a member of the minor nobility in Nottinghamshire. He attended Cambridge university and pursued an academic career as a professor of theology. He received his doctor of divinity degree in 1526. At the age of 37, Cranmer was a bit older than most graduate students of his day. Although there were scholars meeting to study Luther at Cambridge in the 1520's, Cranmer's name does not appear among them. He does seem to have placed more emphasis on the authority of the Bible in matters of theology than on the writings of the medieval church fathers.

In 1529, the modest theology professor suggested that the issue of the king's divorce should be decided by theologians at the leading European universities rather than by the corrupt church courts at Rome. The suggestion came to Henry's attention and he was intrigued by it. Cranmer was authorized to canvass Paris, Padua, Cologne, and even Wittenberg to see what the theologians thought of the matter. He traveled to the universities in person and upon his return, rather than going back to Cambridge, he took a position with the Boleyn family, serving as their chaplain. In 1532, he was sent on an embassy to Emperor Charles V in Germany. While there, he had a great deal of contact with the followers of Luther. He also fell in love, and quietly married the German Lutheran niece of Andreas Osiander, the reformer of Nuremberg.

He had to leave his wife soon after their marriage however. In late 1532, Henry named him as the new Archbishop of Canterbury to succeed Warham who had died over the summer. The clergy in England were still forbidden to marry and Cranmer had to be very discreet about the fact that he was married. He and his wife were separated for several years, and we have very little information about her. It seems that she joined the Archbishop in England sometime during the 1530's. Cranmer and his wife had two children. She lived quietly and very privately at one of his official residences. During the reign of Edward VI, many of Cranmer's associates were surprised to discover that he was married and had been for over ten years.

Although Cranmer complied with Henry's request to pronounce his marriage to Catherine null and void, he did not always automatically accede to Henry's wishes. He opposed Henry most often when the King moved to execute his opponents. Cranmer's appeals were not heeded, but he did speak to the king on behalf of Sir Thomas More, Anne Boleyn, and Thomas Cromwell himself in 1540. Henry was a conservative by nature and both Cranmer and Cromwell were cautious about pushing him too far, too fast. They did succeed in getting the king's approval for editions of the English Bible to be licensed and openly sold after 1538, but they were never able to persuade Henry to embrace Protestant theology. Cromwell and Cranmer, both with Protestant sympathies, were natural allies. Cranmer's ability to hold and keep the king's trust amazed Cromwell who once remarked, "You were born in a happy hour, for do or say what you will, the King will always well take it at your hand."

In spite of his use of Parliament to enforce Catholic orthodoxy, and his differences with Cranmer theologically, King Henry would never listen to accusations of heresy directed against his friend Cranmer. When Cranmer was charged with being a heretic by other bishops around 1540, Henry told him in a private interview, "My chaplain, I have news for you. I know now who is the greatest heretic in Kent." But then Henry appointed Cranmer to head the investigative commission charged with looking into his own heresy! On another occasion, five years later, when members of the King's council were considering charges against Cranmer, Henry sent a message consisting of a single sentence, "I pray you, use not my friends so."

Beginning in 1540, Cranmer began to devote himself to reforming the way church services were conducted. His project was the preparation of an English Prayer Book. At this time, the liturgy used in services throughout England had changed very little in centuries. All prayers and responses were in Latin that few could understand. Luther had produced a service of worship in German in the late 1520's. Calvin was already at work reforming the worship in Geneva so that it was in the language of the French. Cranmer wished to accomplish the same reforms in England. His Book of Common Prayer, when finished, became one of the masterpieces of the English language, almost as influential as the translations done by Tyndale and King James' scholars.

When Henry died in 1547, Cranmer found himself serving on the council named to govern the nation and advise his heir. Young King Edward VI was only ten years old when he succeeded his father. The council was dominated by Protestants rather than Catholics. Leadership was soon assumed by Thomas Hertford who had himself named "Protector" for the young king. Cranmer gave the Protector his support and assisted in the repeal of the Six Articles and the lifting of all restrictions on the printing and selling of English Bibles.

Cranmer used the new freedom offered by the Protector and Prince Edward to implement his reform of worship in the English churches. He began by replacing some of the Latin prayers with prayers in English in 1548. In 1549, a new prayer book with a service entirely in English was approved by Parliament and required to be used in churches throughout England. To the common man in England, the switch from Latin to English must have been stunning. For the first time, each element in the service of worship was understandable and invited his attention, contemplation, and contributed to his theological education.

Cranmer also used the change in government to invite scholars from the continent to move to English universities. Luther himself had died in 1542, but his Wittenberg ally, Melanchthon was invited to accept a post at Cambridge. He declined, but Martin Bucer of Strasburg accepted, since Strasburg had recently been occupied by troops of Charles V and forced to restore the Catholic Mass. Bucer taught theology at Cambridge and assisted Cranmer in revising the English prayer book.

In late 1549, another English nobleman, John Dudley, the Earl of Warwick (he later adopted the title Duke of Northumberland) staged a coup, backed by the more conservative and Catholic opponents of "Protector" Hertford. Cranmer survived by switching his allegiances to the winning side. After Hertford was imprisoned in the tower, Warwick surprised his backers by continuing Protestant reforms and protecting Cranmer.

It soon became apparent, though, that Cranmer had even more serious things to worry about. Fifteen year old King Edward, never a strong child, was not well. By 1552 it was clear that he was dying. Northumberland arranged a marriage between his son and Lady Jane Grey (because Henry VIII was her great-uncle) and persuaded Edward to name her as his heir. But Henry VIII in his will had specified that the succession to the throne should pass from Edward, his only son to Mary, his oldest daughter, and then to Elizabeth his second daughter. When Edward died in 1553, Mary slipped away to East Anglia and rallied support to her claim on the basis of King Henry VIII's will. Lady Jane Grey, sixteen years old, reigned as Queen for nine days before Mary's forces took over in London. She was imprisoned in the tower and later executed for treason along with her husband and her father-in-law.

The accession of Mary Tudor to the throne was not good news for Archbishop Cranmer of Canterbury. As the daughter of a Spanish princess, Mary had been raised as a staunch Roman Catholic. All through the reign of Henry VIII and Edward VI, she had retained a Roman Catholic priest as her chaplain and continued to sponsor the celebration of the mass. Within weeks of her accession to the throne, the Roman Catholic religion was officially reestablished throughout England. Archbishop Cranmer soon found himself in prison, along with five other bishops whom Mary had deposed for their "heretical" views.

In January of 1554, Mary announced that she would marry her cousin, King Philip II of Spain. The Spanish marriage was intensely unpopular in England, for it meant that England would be ruled by a foreign, Spanish king. In the summer of 1554, Sir Thomas Wyatt led a serious rebellion. An armed force of 4,000 marched on London. Mary only barely managed to defeat the rebels. Mary was then persuaded that she must sign the death warrants for Lady Jane Grey and her husband, fearing other rebels who might rally around her claim to the throne.

In 1555, less than two years after her coronation as Queen, Mary began the execution of Protestant heretics. Before she died, Mary was responsible for the deaths of scores of Protestants. For these deaths, she earned the nickname, "Bloody Mary." John Rogers, the associate of Tyndale who had edited the *Thomas Matthew's Bible* was the first to be burned. He was followed shortly by two prominent Protestant bishops, Latimer and Ridley. Latimer and Ridley had been close friends with Cranmer and the three had been imprisoned and tried together. Cranmer was a prisoner in Oxford when the day came for their execution. He watched the proceedings from the roof of the house in which he was lodged. Foxe records that as they were being led to the stake, Ridley faltered. Latimer encouraged him, saying, "Be of good comfort, master Ridley, and play the man; we shall this day light such a candle by God's grace in England as, I trust, shall never be put out."

Thomas Cranmer's turn followed soon after. He had already been tried for heresy and condemned. Apparently terrified of death, he recanted all of his Protestant opinions in the hope that his life would be spared. But Mary and her advisors were adamant that Cranmer must be executed as a heretic, recantation or no. On the day of his execution, he was placed on a stage inside of the church of St. Mary in Oxford, and stood there with tears streaming down his cheeks. When he was allowed an opportunity to speak, he surprised everyone by withdrawing his recantation! He denounced the Pope as the antichrist and the Mass as idolatry. He was quickly pulled off the stage and dragged outside to the ditch where Latimer and Ridley had died. There he was burned at the stake. Before his execution he had promised that he would hold his right hand in the fire to be burned first since he had used it to sign his "false recantations." Foxe's *Book of Martyrs* records that:

> "When the wood was kindled and the fire began to burn near him, stretching out his arm, he put his right hand into the flame, which he held so steadfast and immovable (saving that once with the same hand he wiped his face) that all men might see his hand burned before his body was touched ... Using often the words of Stephen, 'Lord Jesus, receive my spirit;' in the greatness of the flame he gave up the ghost."[31]

Mary did not have long to rule however. She died in the early morning hours of November 1558, having reigned for just six years. She was succeeded by her younger half-sister, the twenty-five year old Queen Elizabeth.

Chapter 28

John Calvin 1509-1564

Jean Cauvin was born on July 10, 1509, as the second of five sons to a minor church official in northern France, in the town of Noyon in Picardy. His father was a notary and legal advocate for the cathedral chapter of Noyon. Calvin's (for this is the way his name has come to be spelled in the English-speaking world) father planned a career in the church for his son. At the age of eleven, Jean was appointed one of the chaplains in the cathedral. Since he was too young to be ordained as a priest, his father hired a substitute to say mass in his place. The appointment as a chaplain meant that young Jean received an income from the church. Those who wished masses to be said were required to give a specified amount to the cathedral. The bishop received a portion of the fees, the cathedral chapter (the "guild" of priests who served in the church) received a portion of the fees, and Jean Calvin's substitute received a portion. The rest was paid as an income to Jean (or in his case, since he was so young, to his father).

Calvin received his early education with private tutors. At the age of ten, his parents arranged for him to move into the home of a local nobleman, and to share lessons with his sons. In 1521, at the age of eleven, Jean moved to Paris to continue his education at the College de la Marche, part of the University of Paris. Years later, he dedicated his commentary on I Thessalonians to his Latin teacher at the College, Mathurin Cordier. After a year, Jean transferred to the College de Montaigu, where Erasmus had studied. He stayed there until he finished his course of studies with a degree as Master of Arts in 1526 at the age of seventeen.

Calvin's progress in his studies at Paris allowed his father to further his career in the church. By 1526, he had obtained two more appointments for his son as priest in parishes near Noyon. Once again substitutes were hired to discharge the day-to-day duties in Jean's place while he remained at Paris. Although by this time Luther and Zwingli had been actively reforming the church for almost ten years, there is nothing in Calvin's writings or behavior to show that he had the least interest in either Protestant or Catholic theology. In fact, Calvin seems to have resolved to abandon his promising ecclesiastical career and to pursue a more lucrative occupation as a lawyer.

In 1526, Calvin left Paris for Orleans and began studies in the law school there. In 1529, he transferred to the University at Bourges to study Roman law, especially the Code of Justinian. Just as Luther's father had, Jean's father made the expensive investment in a copy of the *Corpus Juris* for his son.

As he studied Roman law, Calvin had also acquired in interest in the classical authors of Ancient Rome. At Bourges, in addition to studying law, he was also learning Greek. With his knowledge of Greek he was able to join that small community of scholars who were studying the New Testament in its original language. Sometime between 1530 and 1534, Calvin was converted. He was between twenty-one and twenty-five years old. The details of his conversion are not known by historians. Calvin was a very private person and only once described his conversion in print — in the preface to his commentary on the Psalms. There he says:

> "At first I remained so obstinately addicted to the superstitions of the papacy
> that it would have been hard indeed to have pulled me out of so deep a
> quagmire by a sudden conversion. But God subdued and made teachable a
> heart which, for my age, was far too hardened in such matters. Having
> received some foretaste and knowledge of true piety, I was inflamed with
> such great desire to profit by it that, although I did not give up my other
> studies, I worked only slackly at them. I was wonder-struck, when, before
> the year was out, all those who had some desire for true doctrine ranged
> themselves around me to learn, although I was hardly more than a begin-
> ner myself."[32]

In 1532, at the age of twenty-two, Calvin marked two milestones. First, he completed his legal education and received his degree as a Doctor of Laws. Secondly, he published his first book, a commentary on the essay *On Clemency* by the Roman writer, Seneca. The book displays both the young lawyer Calvin's skill as a humanist and his command of classical Latin. But there is nothing in it that shows any understanding or commitment on the great theological debate of his day.

In 1533, Calvin was in Paris, as a promising young lawyer, perhaps moving towards a career as a professor of the law. One of his good friends and a classmate from his days at the University of Paris, Nicholas Cop, had just been elected Rector. In October, Cop gave an address in which he criticized the Catholic theologians of the university and advocated reform. Although not explicitly identifying himself with Luther, Cop's address led many to suspect he was a Lutheran. A warrant was issued for Cop's arrest by the city council of Paris and he quickly fled, taking refuge in Basel, a city near where the borders of Germany, France and Switzerland meet. Since Calvin was widely known as a close friend of Cop's, he thought it best to flee Paris as well. He headed first for his home in Noyon.

In Noyon, he went to the cathedral and formally resigned his two appointments as parish priest and altar-priest in the cathedral. No explanation was given, but it seems clear that by now, Jean Calvin had chosen to stand with Luther and those who had broken with the Roman Catholic church. From Noyon, Calvin traveled to Angeloume in southwest France, where he stayed with another of his friends from his University of Paris days, Louis du Tillet.

While staying with his friend in Angeloume, Calvin began to work on a defense of the Lutheran or Protestant understanding of the Christian faith. He called the book he was working on, *The Institutes of Christian Religion*.

In October of 1534, the followers and sympathizers of the Lutherans staged a nationwide protest by posting placards in the chief towns throughout France. The placards attacked the Roman Catholic Sacrament of the Mass, calling it a "great, horrible, and unendurable abuse" -- the exact opposite of what Jesus had intended at the Last Supper. King Francis I was outraged. He ordered royal officials everyone to find the "Lutherans" and arrest them. Two hundred Protestants were captured. Over the next three months, twenty Protestants were executed, including one of Calvin's friends in Paris, Etienne de la Forge.

Calvin and his friend, du Tillet, decided that it was too dangerous to stay in France, that they must leave and join their friend Nicholas Cop in exile. In January, 1535, they arrived in Basel. There they joined the small community of French, Protestant exiles in the prosperous German city. Basel had only recently, in 1529, by a formal vote of the city council, reformed its churches along Protestant lines. As a learned young lawyer and humanist, Calvin quickly found employment as a writer and editor. He worked as an assistant to another French humanist, Pierre Robert as he translated the Bible into French. Here his skill with both Latin and Greek proved useful. The time in Basel also gave him opportunity to further his study of Hebrew. Calvin knew that mastering Hebrew would be important if he was to understand the Scriptures fully.

In addition to translation work and language study, Calvin also continued work on his own writings. In March of 1536 only a little more than a year after he fled from France to Basel, a local printer published a volume by the twenty-seven year old Jean Calvin titled *The Institutes of Christian Religion*. Although the book opened with a dedication to King Francis I of France, its purpose was not to flatter. In the dedication, Calvin criticized the king for his persecution of the Protestants in France. He defended the actions of the Protestants in the affair of the placards. Calvin begged the King not just to tolerate the Protestants, but to examine their teaching closely. What Calvin wanted from the King was not toleration, but recognition that the Protestants are the true defenders of Christianity. He argued that it was the Roman Catholic Church which had departed from the faith of the fathers and become heretical.

Calvin's summary of Christianity was divided into six chapters: On the Law; On Faith; On Prayer; On the Sacraments; On False Sacraments; On Christian Liberty and Church and State Authority. The book was immediately acclaimed and admired by Protestant theologians everywhere, including Luther. Great things were expected in the future from the promising young theologian, humanist, lawyer, and now, successful author.

In 1536, Calvin, seeking a place where he could pursue his study and writing, made a brief trip to Ferrarra, Italy. The Duke of Ferrarra's French wife had offered refuge to a number of French Protestants. It turned out that the Duchess was unable to prevent the Catholic church from arresting those charged with heresy. Calvin returned to Basel and then decided to return to Paris. King Francis I had halted all persecution of Protestants in France — but only temporarily. He gave assurances that they would not be disturbed for six months. At the end of that time, if they had not been reconciled to the Roman Catholic Church, they would be subject to all the penalties of heresy — excommunication from the church and execution by the civil authorities.

Calvin used the six months respite to return to Paris and conclude family business left unsettled after his father's death in 1531. Before the six months grace could expire, Calvin left Paris to return to Basel. Traveling with him were one of his brothers, his half-sister, and several friends. They were forced to take a long detour to the south, to avoid the large army which Francis I was assembling near the border between France and Germany.

Thus it was, that in the Fall of 1536, they stopped briefly in the city of Geneva. While there, Calvin was approached by an acquaintance from his stay in Basel, William Farel. Farel knew of the young lawyer's scholarly abilities. He had only recently helped to win the city of Geneva to the Protestant cause. He asked the young Jean Calvin to stay in the city and help to complete the reform of the church there.

At first Calvin refused, protesting that he was a scholar and a writer. He wished for no office. He did not want to be a preacher or reformer. At this Farel became angry. He said that if Calvin refused to help him complete the reforms in Geneva, that God would curse Calvin's quiet, scholarly life and he would never find peace to write.

The city of Geneva had been ruled by a bishop and its latest had been notoriously corrupt and immoral. The city council and citizens had forced him to flee the city in 1534. Protestant preachers from other Swiss cities were invited to come and proclaim their doctrine in the city. Farel had been one of those invited to teach. By 1535, the city council had voted to reform the churches of the city and adopt practices along the lines of other Swiss Protestant cities.

Farel wanted Calvin's help in Geneva. He knew that, while the city council had voted to adopt reforms, the population of the city had as yet, little knowledge of what the Bible taught about the Christian life. Calvin agreed to help Farel. He began by preaching and teaching from the letters of Paul, beginning with Romans, in the main church in the city, St. Pierre's.

In 1537, the city council of Geneva elected Calvin and William Farel as the official town preachers. The young, twenty-eight year old lawyer-theologian patiently preached through the New Testament. In his sermons, he carefully explained the application of Scripture both to practices in the church, and to the everyday life of the Christian.

Calvin and Farel drew up a set of ordinances to govern the reformed churches of Geneva and a confession of faith. Both were adopted by the city council and all citizens and inhabitants were required to subscribe to the confession. There was opposition. Some suspected that Farel and Calvin, because they were French, might have secret ties to the king of France. Geneva was jealous of her newly won independence and suspicious that her powerful neighbors wished to annex the city. That Calvin would be an agent of the French king was extremely unlikely. He had been banished from France and was hardly in the king's favor. Others in Geneva were simply jealous of Calvin and Farel's influence and resistant to change.

The opposition to Calvin and Farel came to a climax just before Easter of 1538. Both were exiled from Geneva. Farel was soon called to the Swiss city of Neuchatel and asked to lead the reform of the churches there. Calvin returned first to Basel. Then, at the invitation of Martin Bucer of Strasburg, he moved to that important Imperial city to become pastor to a congregation of French refugees. It was a position he held for three years, from 1538 to 1541.

In Strasburg, he tended to his flock as a pastor. He preached, married, baptized, buried and counseled. He also earned a little as a private tutor to students in the Academy — helping them with the finer points of Latin, Greek, and Hebrew grammar. From time to time, he even used his legal expertise to draw up briefs on behalf of a paying client. He also completed an expanded and revised edition of *The Institutes of the Christian Religion* and a *Commentary on the Book of Romans*.

While living in Strasburg, Calvin married a widow with 3 children. Jean and Idelette had one child in 1542, but he lived only a few days. Idelette died in 1549.

Meanwhile, things were not well in Geneva. The city was divided over what course to pursue with regard to religion. Cardinal Sadoleto wrote an appeal, urging the people of Geneva to return home to Rome. Calvin, in Strasburg, composed a *Reply to Sadoleto*. In his reply, he argued that the church is not the visible bureaucracy, but the communion of all believers. Salvation, he reminded them, does not come through the sacraments of the Roman Catholic Church, but by faith alone, directly to each believer.

1541 brought a change of councilors in Geneva. In part, impressed by his *Reply to Sadoleto*, in part, dissatisfied with those who had tried to take his place since 1538, the city council of Geneva wanted Calvin back. Calvin at first resisted. He was happily settled in Strasburg even though his financial circumstances were not the best. His duties allowed him time for study and scholarship. His memories of Geneva were not altogether favorable. But the representatives sent to Strasburg by the council were insistent -- Geneva needed him. They begged him to return and to complete the reform of the church. Calvin at last, consented. He and his wife, and her three children packed up and set off to the city on the lake. Once there, Calvin set to work organizing, reforming, and implementing the governance of the churches in Geneva. He insisted, as before, that the church was to be independent of the secular authorities, ruled by elders and deacons who would be chosen by the congregations. The elders and deacons in turn would be responsible for selecting preachers and teachers.

On his first Sunday back in Geneva, Calvin resumed preaching at the passage he had finished before his exile in 1538. His practice was to preach twice on Sundays, and on Mondays, Wednesdays, and Fridays. His preaching was expository, moving methodically, verse by verse through whole books of the Bible. On Sundays he preached from the New Testament; on weekdays from the Old. Beginning in 1549, the Society of French Refuges in Geneva hired a notary who transcribed Calvin's sermons using a system of shorthand. Over 2,000 of his sermons were transcribed and are still available, in bound sets, in the Geneva archives. Although Calvin was a reserved and private individual, his sermons were described by his hearers as lively and passionate. He was, by all accounts, a gifted orator.

Calvin's life in Geneva was devoted to the duties of a pastor — above all preaching, but also writing. He wrote commentaries on I Corinthians (1546), II Corinthians (1547), Galatians, Ephesians, Philippians, Colossians (1548), I & II Timothy (1548), Titus and Hebrews (1549), I & II Thessalonians and Philemon (1550), Acts (in 2 vol.—1552), and the Gospel of John (1553).

Calvin was not a citizen of Geneva, and held no position in its secular government. He was the appointed town preacher, and teacher of Christian doctrine. He had tremendous influence, but no official position in the church consistory. The consistory was composed of the company of pastors of all the congregations of the city, a number ranging from nine to nineteen, along with twelve lay elders appointed by the town council. This body was also called the presbytery.

The consistory exercised discipline within the church. It could admonish and call for public repentance within the church. It could even excommunicate an unrepentant sinner from all church services. But the secular city council and city courts meted out all other punishments. Both groups frequently consulted Calvin, for both his theological as well as his legal opinions. The consistory met weekly to deal with issues of moral behavior by members of the church congregations. They excommunicated for a variety of offenses ranging from wife beating, public quarreling and brawling, to drunkenness, gambling, and fornication.

Two events in the 1540's served to focus attention on Calvin and Geneva as the leader of the Protestant reform movement. In 1546, came the news from Wittenberg that Luther had died. Zwingli had died fifteen years earlier. Leadership in Wittenberg and Zurich had passed to a second generation — Melanchthon and Bullinger. Calvin was more than their equal in ability and prestige. In 1547, Emperor Charles V defeated the German Protestant Princes at Muhlberg. The German states and cities, including Strasburg, were required by the Emperor to re-institute Catholic worship including the Mass. They were also required to recognize the authority of Roman Catholic bishops and church courts.

Geneva emerged in this decade as the leader of the Protestant movement. The influence of Geneva and the example of its churches on the Protestants in France was immense. Calvin carried on a large correspondence with friends and sympathizers for many years. He never gave up hope that the whole of France might be reformed along the lines he had pioneered in Geneva. Many French Protestants sought refuge in Geneva. After spending time there and becoming acquainted with Calvin's reforms, many returned to France as underground missionaries for the Protestant cause. As their little underground groups prospered and grew, they often wrote to Calvin asking for guidance and very often begging him to send them a minister of the Gospel.

In 1559, the Geneva Academy was founded to train pastors and preachers. The Academy, which later became the University of Geneva, attracted students from all over Europe — but especially from France, the Netherlands, and England. Between the years 1553 and 1558 a large number of Protestant refugees came to Geneva from England, fleeing the persecutions of the Roman Catholic "Bloody" Mary. But the graduates of the Academy most often returned to their homelands where they organized new Reformed churches.

Calvin's followers in France came to be known as Hugenots. The word is derived from the German word for "confederate" (*Eidgenossen*) a term which identified those whose sympathies lay with the Swiss Confederation of Cantons.

In 1553, a Spaniard named Michael Servetus stopped briefly in Geneva on his way from France to Naples. He attended one of the services at which Calvin was preaching. Calvin recognized him and denounced him publicly as a heretic. Servetus was arrested and ordered to be tried before the Geneva city council. Calvin and Servetus had known each other for sixteen years. Servetus had published, as a brash and arrogant young man, a treatise titled *On the Errors of the Trinity*. In his book he argued that the concept of the Trinity of God was nowhere to be found in the Bible. Servetus had lived for some years under an assumed name in France, where his learning allowed him to earn a living as a physician. He had begun a correspondence with Calvin by challenging some of Calvin's teaching on the Trinity. Calvin replied to his letters and sent him a copy of the Institutes. Servetus returned the book with his own comments challenging and criticizing Calvin's doctrines in the margin. In 1553, he was jailed in France, though he managed to escape before the court could pronounce sentence. After his departure, he was condemned as a heretic and sentenced to be executed — since he had escaped, he was burned in effigy, along with copies of his books.

His decision to stop in Geneva on his flight towards Italy was ill-advised. After a brief trial in which Calvin attempted, in vain, to persuade him to alter his opinions, he was condemned by the city council to be burned at the stake. Calvin and other ministers asked that he be beheaded instead of burned, but the council refused. The sentence was carried out the next day.

The following year, Calvin wrote an essay entitled *Defense of the Orthodox Trinity Against the Errors of Michael Servetus*. The same year, Sebastian Castellio, a humanist colleague of Calvin's, now living in Basel, wrote a public rebuke of Calvin's behavior in the Servetus case called, *Concerning Heretics, Whether They Are to Be Persecuted and How They Are to Be Treated*. While admitting that Servetus was in error (and arrogant and irritating to boot), he argued strongly against the persecution of men because of their religious beliefs. He particularly denounced the persecution of the Anabaptists by both Catholic and Protestant authorities. He lamented how displeased Christ would be were he to return and find his supposed followers quarreling, fighting, and killing each other.

Calvin did not respond.

In 1551, Calvin had published the first of his commentaries on the Old Testament, on the book of *Isaiah* — dedicated to King Edward VI of England. In 1554, he published a commentary on *Genesis*. *Hosea* was published in 1557. A revised version of *Isaiah* was published in 1559 (dedicated to Queen Elizabeth of England) along with a volume on the *Minor Prophets*. *Daniel* appeared in 1561, *Jeremiah and Lamentations* in 1563. After he died in 1564, two volumes appeared posthumously on *Joshua* and *Ezekiel*. Had he lived longer, he would have published commentaries on every book of the Bible. He also completed, in 1559, another major expansion and revision of *The Institutes of the Christian Religion*, which had now expanded to four volumes and eighty chapters. The treatment of all topics was expanded, but especially the section on the Governance of the church, which had been 1/3 of a chapter in 1536, was now covered in twelve separate chapters.

In the winter of 1558-59, Calvin was seriously ill and even when he recovered, he seemed greatly weakened. Although he continued to preach and to write and to meet regularly with the consistory and the company of pastors, it was clear that his health was failing. In the Spring of 1564, he preached his last series of sermons from the pulpit of St. Pierre's in Geneva. He died in May of that year and, at his own request, was buried in an unmarked grave in the common cemetery of Geneva.

Just before his death, the company of pastors met with him in his house. His final words to them included this:

> "... I have had many infirmities which you have been obliged to bear with, and what is more, all I have done has been worth nothing. The ungodly will greedily seize upon this word, but I say it again that all I have done has been worth nothing, and that I am a miserable creature. But certainly I can say this, that I have willed what is good, that my vices have always displeased me, and that the root of the fear of God has been in my heart; and you may say that the disposition was good; and I pray you that the evil be forgiven me, and if there was any good, that you conform yourselves to it and make it an example.
>
> As to my doctrine, I have taught faithfully, and God has given me grace to write what I have written as faithfully as it was in my power. I have not falsi-

fied a single passage of the Scriptures, nor given it a wrong interpretation to the best of my knowledge; and though I might have introduced subtle senses, had I studied subtlety, I cast that temptation under my feet and always aimed at simplicity.

I have written nothing out of hatred to any one, but I have always faithfully propounded what I esteemed to be for the glory of God."[33]

In his final letter to his friend and fellow minister, William Farel, the man who had first persuaded him to leave a life of scholarship and take up the responsibility of reforming the churches of Geneva, Calvin wrote:

"Since it is God's will that you should outlive me, remember our friendship. It was useful to God's Church and its fruits await us in heaven. I do not want you to tire yourself on my account. I draw my breath with difficulty and expect each moment to breathe my last. It is enough that I live and die for Christ, who is to all his followers a gain both in life and in death."[34]

Chapter 29

John Knox 1514-1572

"All service invented by the brain of man in the religion of God, without his express command, is idolatry. The Mass is invented by the brain of man without the command of God; therefore it is idolatry."
— **John Knox to Bishop Tunstall of Durham, 1550**

John Knox was born in 1514 in a the small town of Haddington, just east of Edinburgh. He attended school in Haddington where he learned classical Latin and entered St. Andrew's University in 1529. At the University, he studied law and then theology. In 1536, he was ordained as a priest and accepted a position as tutor to the sons of a local member of the nobility in his home of Haddington. In his spare time, he began reading the many writings of the reformers — Luther, Zwingli, and the Institutes of Christian Religion, lately published in Strasburg by the French Lawyer-Theologian, John Calvin. He also found time to study the new English Bibles by Tyndale and others. The details of his conversion to the Protestant cause are not known to historians. On his death-bed, he asked his wife to read John 18 to him, describing it as the passage "where I first cast my anchor."

In 1545, the Protestant preacher George Wishart came to Haddington and stayed with the family whose sons Knox was tutoring. Knox was much impressed with Wishart and decided to accompany him as he traveled through southern Scotland preaching and teaching. For five weeks, Knox and Wishart traveled together. While Wishart preached, Knox stood guard beside him, holding a large two-handed, Scottish sword.

When the Catholic Archbishop Cardinal Beaton ordered Wishart's arrest in 1546, Wishart sent his followers and friends, including Knox away, saying "One is sufficient for a sacrifice." Wishart surrendered to the authorities, was tried as a heretic, convicted and executed on March 1st at St. Andrews, Scotland. His execution at the hands of Cardinal Beaton outraged many. In his short career, Wishart had had a major impact upon not only the common people, but many of the lairds and clan leaders of southern Scotland. Cardinal Beaton's own reputation was notorious, for he had fathered ten illegitimate children.

Two months after Wishart's death, a small group of Scots noblemen avenged him by breaking into the Archbishop's residence and stabbing him to death. The regent of Scotland immediately moved to apprehend the assassins, who were besieged in the Archbishop's residence, the castle of St. Andrews. Although Knox had not been a participant in the plot, he joined the "Castilians" (as they were called) shortly after the siege began. It was during his stay in St. Andrews, that his countrymen called upon him to accept the office of preacher and to proclaim the gospel. Knox declined at first, but within a week, while attending services at a parish church in St. Andrews, he heard a catholic priest defending the Roman church as the one, true, bride of Christ. Knox immediately leapt to his feet and challenged the priest, saying "The Roman Church is no bride of Christ, but a harlot!" The crowd began to angrily demand that Knox prove his charge. Knox returned the following week and preached a sermon on that very theme, winning over many of the congregation.

The Castilians in St. Andrews were not strong enough to defy the regent for long however. In the summer of 1547, a year after the assassination of the Archbishop, reinforcements arrived from France and the rebels were forced to surrender. All of the Castilians were taken to France and imprisoned. Many, including Knox, were sentenced to serve in the French fleet as galley slaves. Knox spent eighteen months doing the backbreaking labor of rowing a heavy warship before he was freed. His freedom came because of the intervention of the Protestant government of England under King Edward VI and Protector Somerset.

Knox sailed from captivity in France to freedom in England. He spent two years as a preacher in Northern England, near the border with Scotland. It was here that he made the celebrated remark to Bishop Tunstall of Durham which was quoted at the beginning of the chapter. In 1551, Knox moved to London, where he was appointed one of the king's royal chaplains. He continued his preaching and also assisted Archbishop Cranmer in the revision of the Book of Common Prayer. Knox was offered some prominent positions in the Anglican Church, including Bishop of Rochester, but he turned them down.

Knox became engaged in the Spring of 1553, but political developments in England forced him to postpone his plans for marriage. King Edward VI died in the summer of 1553, and Queen Mary came to the throne. Her opposition to the "Protestant heresy" was well known. By the end of the year, Knox had left England. He traveled first to Geneva, where he met with John Calvin, who encouraged him to continue his calling to preach and lead. On

1560 Geneva Bible in English
A project John Knox worked on

Calvin's advice, he accepted a call from a group of English refugees in Frankfurt am Main to be the pastor of their congregation of about two hundred. Knox declined to use the Edwardian Book of Common Prayer, drawing up his own revised order of worship and reformulated prayers instead. Many of the refugees found this unacceptable and a split soon developed. Knox's supporters were a minority and the majority succeeded in having him removed from the pulpit in the summer of 1555. Knox left Frankfurt in disgust and returned to Geneva, where Calvin appointed him pastor for the English refugees there.

Many of his friends in Scotland were begging him to return. He responded by spending the winter of 1555-56 on a preaching tour through the lowlands. The Catholic bishops of Scotland were alarmed at his success in organizing reformed congregations and issued warrants for his arrest. Once again, he fled the country, and returned to Geneva. Knox was troubled by the hostility to the gospel displayed by Queen Mary of England and Queen Mary, Regent of Scotland. The persecution of Protestants by bloody Mary was shocking and disheartening to everyone in Geneva. The equally hostile attitude displayed by Mary of Guise, widow of King James V and regent of Scotland, angered Knox as well. In 1558 he published his most notorious tract, The First Blast of the Trumpet Against the Monstrous Regiment of Women. His argument was that no woman could be a legitimate ruler. He based his arguments upon selected passages from the Bible and the early church fathers.

Knox's friends were dismayed by the tract. Most disagreed with it and even those who did not thought it tactically very unwise. Calvin banned the tract in Geneva. The problem, he said, was not that the rulers of England and Scotland were women, but that they were opposed to the Gospel. The problems caused by the tract became even worse for Knox when Queen Mary died in November of 1558, only a few months after the tract's publication. "Bloody" Mary was succeeded by Queen Elizabeth, who invited the Protestant exiles to return to England. Knox did not approve of Elizabeth's half-hearted embrace of Protestantism, calling her "neither good Protestant nor yet resolute Papist." Knox was certainly not Elizabeth's favorite preacher either.

Knox left Geneva and returned to Scotland in 1559 at the invitation of the leaders of the Protestant "Lords of the Congregation." These Lords were also opposed to the regency of Mary of Guise. Knox began at Perth where he denounced Catholic idolatry as an example of trusting in works rather than faith. When he finished preaching, a riot broke out as parishioners smashed altars and images throughout the church and then moved to other chapels in the town.

The "Lords of the Congregation" defeated the forces of Mary of Guise in the summer of 1560 and she agreed to withdraw from the Kingdom. The Scottish Parliament met later that month in Edinburgh and invited Knox to preach at a great thanksgiving service at St. Gile's in Edinburgh. The Parliament further directed Knox to head a commission to draw up a liturgy and constitution for the Scottish church. This liturgy was based on the service Knox had written during his time in Frankfurt and Geneva. It was approved and adopted by the Scottish Parliament by the end of the year.

In 1560, Mary of Guise, regent of Scotland, died. That same year, her son-in-law, King Francis II of France also died. This left her daughter, also named Mary, as the former Queen of France, but now the actual Queen of Scotland. Mary chose to return from France to Scotland where she ruled as Mary, Queen of Scots. Mary was grudgingly accepted by the Lords of the Congregation when she promised to respect the reforms of the Scottish Church, but she reserved the right to worship privately as a Catholic. Knox attacked her from the pulpit at St. Giles in Edinburgh almost as soon as she arrived. Knox and Mary disliked each other from the beginning and matters only worsened over time. He denounced her plan to marry the heir to the Spanish Crown, and she demanded that he cease interfering in her private affairs.

In 1565, Mary did marry, not the Spanish prince, but her own English first cousin, Henry Stuart, Lord Darnley. The next year she gave birth to a son, the future James VI of Scotland and James I of England. Scarcely a year after the birth of her son, her jealous husband murdered her private secretary, David Riccio, whom he suspected of having an affair with Mary. Mary, in turn, plotted the murder of her husband. Darnley was killed the following year when a cottage he was staying in was blown up by a barrel of strategically placed gunpowder. Mary then escaped from Edinburgh, joined her husband's murderer, James Hepburn, and married him.

Knox and all of Scotland were outraged. In June of 1567, Mary was captured by the forces of the Lords of the Congregation and forced to abdicate in favor of her 13-month old son. A year later, she escaped her house arrest, and fled to England, leaving her young son to be raised as a good Scots Presbyterian by Knox and the Scottish Lords. The son of Mary, Queen of Scots grew up to be King James VI of Scotland, and after Queen Elizabeth died, King James I of England. Mary did not fare so well. She was given refuge by her cousin Queen Elizabeth, but was watched closely. She repeatedly involved herself in plots to overthrow Elizabeth. Eventually, after a twenty year sojourn in England, Elizabeth had her executed in 1588.

Knox continued to preach at St. Giles in Scotland, but by the late 1560's his health was failing. He preached his last sermon on November 9th, 1572 and died five days later at the age of 58. By his tenacious, persistent efforts, Knox succeeded in reforming the Church of Scotland and brought it into conformity with the doctrines and form of government he had learned from Calvin in Geneva. The principle of self-governing congregations, with lay representatives at every level, would have a profound impact over the next several centuries on the way people thought about both church and civil government in Scotland, in England, and in England's colonies in North America.

Bibliography

The Renaissance

History of Art, H.W. Janson, Prentice-Hall, 1962

The Lives of the Artists, Giorgio Vasari, trans. by Bondanell, Oxford University Press, 1991

Renaissance Profiles, edited by J.H.Plumb, Harper & Row, 1961

Eight Philosophers of the Italian Renaissance, Paul O. Kristeller, Stanford University Press, 1964

Selected Sonnets, Odes, and Letters, Petrarch, edited by Thomas G. Bergin, AHM Publishing, 1966

Renaissance Lives, Theodore K. Rabb, Random House, 1993

Renaissance Characters, edited by Eugenio Garin, University of Chicago Press, 1991

The Civilization of Europe in the Renaissance, John Hale, Atheneum, 1994

A Concise Encyclopaedia of the Italian Renaissance, edited by J.R. Hale, Oxford University Press, 1981

The House of Medici: Its Rise and Fall, Christopher Hibbert, Morrow, 1974

Leonardo Da Vinci, Francesca Romei, Peter Bedrick Books, 1994

Cesare Borgia, John Haney, Chelsea House Publishers, 1987

The Italian Renaissance, Paul Robert Walker, Facts on File, 1995

Albrecht Dürer: A Biography, Jane Hutchinson, Princeton University Press, 1990

Michelangelo, Richard McLanathan, Harry N. Abrams, Inc., Publishers, 1993

The Reformation

The Protestant Reformation: 1517-1559, Lewis W. Spitz, Harper & Row, 1985

The Renaissance and Reformation Movements, Lewis W. Spitz, Rand McNally, 1971

Europe In Transition: 1300-1520, Wallace K. Ferguson, Houghton Mifflin, 1962

The Age of Reform: 1250-1550, Steven Ozment, Yale University Press, 1980

Reformation Europe: 1517-1559, G.R. Elton, Harper & Row, 1963

The Radical Reformation, (third edition) George H. Williams, Sixteenth Century Journal Publishers, 1992

Here I Stand: A Life of Martin Luther, Roland H. Bainton, Abingdon Press, 1950

Luther's Progress to the Diet of Worms, E. Gordon Rupp, Harper Torchbook, 1968

Luther: Man between God and the Devil, Heiko A. Oberman, Yale University Press, 1989

Thomas Muentzer, a Destroyer of the Godless, Abraham Friesen, University of California Press, 1990

The Life and Thought of Michael Sattler, C. Arnold Snyder, Herald Press, 1984

The Life of Sir Thomas More, William Roper, Templegate Publishers,

William Tyndale: A Biography, David Daniell, Yale University Press, 1994

Thomas Cranmer, Diarmaid MacCulloch, Yale University Press, 1996

John Calvin, T.H.L. Parker, J.M.Dent & Sons, 1975

A Life of John Calvin, Alister E. McGrath, Baker Book House, 1990

The English Reformation, A.G. Dickens, Schocken Books, 1964

This Realm of England, Lacey Baldwin Smith, D.C.Heath & Co., 1976

Endnotes

1 quoted in Spitz, *The Renaissance and Reformation Movements*, p. 144

2 quoted in Rabb, *Renaissance Lives*, p. 13

3 quoted in Rabb, *Renaissance Lives*, p. 18

4 from *Selected Sonnets, Odes, and Letters of Petrarch*, edited by Thomas G. Bergin, p. 98

5 quoted in Vasari, *The Lives of the Artists*, translated by Bondanella, p. 36

6 Ibid, p. 110

7 quoted in Hibbert, *The House of Medici*, p. 40

8 Ibid, p. 149

9 Ibid, p. 163

10 quoted in Vasari, *The Lives of the Artists*, translated by Bondanella, p. 295

11 quoted in Haney, *Cesare Borgia*, p. 45

12 Garrett Mattingly, *Renaissance Profiles*, p. 31-32

13 quoted in Hibbert, *The House of Medici*, p. 204

14 quoted in Hutchinson, *Albrecht Dürer*, p. 21

15 Ibid, p. 124

16 Ibid, p. 165

17 quoted in Bainton, *Here I Stand*, p. 92

18 quoted in Rupp, *Luther's Progress*, p. 27

19 quoted in Bainton, *Here I Stand*, p. 144

20 Ibid, p. 226

21 Ibid, p. 226

22 Ibid, p. 228

23 Ibid, p. 229

24 Ibid, p. 229

25 Ibid, p. 165-166

26 quoted in Spitz, *The Protestant Reformation*, p. 99

27 January 1510, a daughter, stillborn; January 1511, a son who lived for six weeks; November 1513, a son, stillborn; December 1514, a son, stillborn; February, 1516, a daughter, the Princess Mary; November, 1518, a daughter, stillborn. From Henry Churchyard's Royal Genealogies, (http://ftp.cac.psu.edu/~saw/royal/royalgen.html)

28 quoted in Roper, *The Life of Sir Thomas More*, p. 106

29 Ibid, p. 125

30 quoted in Daniell, *William Tyndale*, p. 79

31 quoted in Maculloch, *Thomas Cranmer*, p. 603

32 quoted in Ozment, *The Age of Reform*, p. 355

33 quoted in Parker, *John Calvin*, p. 154

34 Ibid, p. 155

Acknowledgments

Cover: *Photograph of Florence* by Tad Crisp; *Photograph of a 1560 Geneva Bible* by Tad Crisp - our thanks to Thomas Nelson Publishers of Nashville, TN for permission to photograph their Bible.

Page 3: *Sketch of Petrarch by one of his friends*; taken from *Petrarch* by James Harvey Robinson, G.P. Putnam's Sons, 1898; author's collection

Page 10: *Madonna* by Cimabue (Uffizi, Florence, Italy); *Madonna* by Giotto (Uffizi, Florence, Italy); *St. Francis* by Giotto (Upper Church of San Francesco at Assisi); all courtesy Carol Gerten-Jackson (http://www.bod.net/Cjackson)

Page 11: *Giotto's Bell Tower* courtesy Firenze Online (http://www.fionline.it)

Page 12: *Lamentation* by Giotto; Cappella dell'Arena, Padua, Italy; courtesy the WebMuseum (http://sunsite.unc.edu/wm/) and curator, Nicolas Pioch

Page 14: *Photograph of the Duomo* by Tad Crisp

Page 17: *Reconstruction of the Dome* courtesy David Gabriel, Harvard Graduate School of Design (http://www.gsd.harvard.edu/~gsd96dcg/dome.html); *Photograph of the Duomo* by Tad Crisp

Page 21: *Portrait of Cosimo* by Bronzino; Museo Mediceo, Florence, Italy; courtesy Scala/Art Resource, NY

Page 25: *The Adoration of the Magi* by Fra Angelico; Museo San Marco in Florence, Italy; courtesy Carol Gerten-Jackson (http://www.bod.net/Cjackson)

Page 25: *Madonna* by Fra Filippo Lippi; Uffizi, Florence, Italy; courtesy Carol Gerten-Jackson (http://www.bod.net/Cjackson)

Page 26: *The Adoration of the Magi* by Botticelli; Uffizi, Florence, Italy; courtesy Mark Harden and the texas.net Museum of Art (http://lonestar.texas.net/~mharden)

Page 27: Detail from *The Adoration of the Magi by Botticelli*; Uffizi, Florence, Italy; courtesy Mark Harden and the texas.net Museum of Art (http://lonestar.texas.net/~mharden)

Page 33: *Adoration of the Magi* by Fra Filippino Lippi; National Gallery at London, England; courtesy of Carol Gerten-Jackson (http://www.bod.net/Cjackson)

Page 35: *Portrait of Girolamo Savonarola* by Fra Bartolomeo; Museo di San Marco, Florence, Italy; courtesy Scala/Art Resource, NY

Page 39: Detail from *The Adoration of the Magi* by Botticelli, presumed self-portrait of the artist; Uffizi, Florence, Italy; courtesy of Scala/Art Resource

Page 40: *Fortitude* by Botticelli; Uffizi, Florence, Italy; courtesy of Carol Gerten-Jackson (http://www.bod.net/Cjackson)

Page 40: *La Primavera* by Botticelli; Uffizi, Florence, Italy; courtesy of Carol Gerten-Jackson (http://www.bod.net/Cjackson)

Page 41: *The Daughters of Jethro*, from *Scenes from the Life of Moses* by Botticelli; Sistine Chapel, Rome, Italy; courtesy of Carol Gerten-Jackson (http://www.bod.net/Cjackson)

Page 41: *The Mystic Nativity* by Botticelli; National Gallery in London, England; courtesy of Carol Gerten-Jackson (http://www.bod.net/Cjackson)

Page 43: *Self Portrait* by Leonardo da Vinci; National Gallery at Turin, Italy; courtesy of Carol Gerten-Jackson (http://www.bod.net/Cjackson)

Page 44: *The Baptism of Christ* by, Andrea della Verrocchio(with Leonardo da Vinci); Uffizi, Florence, Italy; courtesy Carol Gerten-Jackson (http://www.bod.net/Cjackson)

Page 46: *The Last Supper* by Leonardo da Vinci; Convent of Santa Maria delle Grazie (Refectory), Milan, Italy; courtesy the WebMuseum (http://sunsite.unc.edu/wm/) and curator, Nicolas Pioch

Page 47: *La Gioconda (Mona Lisa)* by Leonardo da Vinci; The Louvre, Paris, France; courtesy of Corel Photo Library

Page 49: *Portrait of Michelangelo* by Marcello Venusti; Casa Buonarroti, Florence, Italy; courtesy Alinari/Art Resource, NY

Page 50: *The Vatican Pieta* by Michelangelo; Rome, Italy; courtesy Tad Crisp

Page 51: *The David* by Michelangelo; Galleria dell'Accademia, Florence, Italy; courtesy Carol Gerten-Jackson (http://www.bod.net/Cjackson)

Page 52: *The Creation of Adam* by Michelangelo; Sistine Chapel, Rome, Italy; courtesy Mark Harden and the texas.net Museum of Art (http://lonestar.texas.net/~mharden)

Page 52: *The Last Judgement* by Michelangelo; Sistine Chapel, Rome, Italy; courtesy Mark Harden and the texas.net Museum of Art (http://lonestar.texas.net/~mharden)

Page 53: *St. Peter's Basilica*; Rome, Italy; courtesy Tad Crisp

Page 53: *The Deposition* by Michelangelo; Santa Maria del Fiore, Florence, Italy; courtesy Carol Gerten-Jackson (http://www.bod.net/Cjackson)

Page 54: *The Ceiling of the Sistine Chapel* by Michelangelo, Rome, Italy; courtesy Mark Harden and the texas.net Museum of Art (http://lonestar.texas.net/~mharden)

Page 55: *Portrait of Cesare Borgia*, anonymous; Palazzo Venezia, Rome, Italy; courtesy Scala/Art Resource, NY

Page 63: *Portrait of Niccolo Machiavelli* by Santi di Tito; Palazzo Vecchio, Florence, Italy; courtesy Erich Lessing/Art Resource, NY

Page 67: *Pope Leo X* by Raphael; Uffizi, Florence, Italy; courtesy the WebMuseum (http://sunsite.unc.edu/wm/) and curator, Nicolas Pioch

Page 73: *Portrait of Erasmus* by Albrecht Dürer; The Louvre, Paris, France; courtesy Carol Gerten-Jackson (http://www.bod.net/Cjackson)

Page 75: *Portrait of Erasmus* by Hans Holbein the Younger; courtesy Mark Harden and the texas.net Museum of Art (http://lonestar.texas.net/~mharden)

Page 79: wood engraving of Wyclif, after an original in the collection of the Duke of Dorset, printed in D'Aubigné, History of the Reformation, Putnam & Sons, 1872 (author's collection)

Page 82: Detail from *Wyclif reading his Bible to John of Gaunt*, Ford Madox Brown; National Gallery, London, England; Courtesy Art Resource, NY

Page 83: wood engraving of Hus, artist unknown, printed in Great Men and Famous Women, Selmar Hess Publishers, 1894 (author's collection)

Page 86: Execution of Hus, wood engraving by C.G. Hellquist, printed in Great Men and Famous Women, Selmar Hess Publishers, 1894 (author's collection)

Page 87: *Portrait of Martin Luther* by Lucas Cranach the Elder; Uffizi, Florence, Italy; courtesy Scala/Art Resource, NY

Page 91: wood engraving of Frederick of Saxony, artist unknown, printed in D'Aubigné, History of the Reformation, Putnam & Sons, 1872 (author's collection)

Page 96: *Portrait of Katarina von Bora* by Lucas Cranach the Elder;Uffizi, Florence, Italy; courtesy Scala/Art Resource, NY

Page 98: Victory in Death, steel engraving, artist unknown, printed in D'Aubigné, History of the Reformation, Putnam & Sons, 1872 (author's collection)

Page 99: *Portrait of Charles V* by Titian;Alte Pinakothek, Munich, Germany; courtesy Carol Gerten-Jackson (http://www.bod.net/Cjackson)

Page 102: *Emperor Charles V at Mühlenberg* by Titian; Museo del Prado, Madrid, Spain; courtesy Erich Lessing/Art Resource, NY

Page 105: *Self-portrait at 26* by Albrecht Dürer; Museo del Prado, Madrid, Spain; courtesy Corel Photo Library

Page 106: *Self-portrait at 22* by Albrecht Dürer; The Louvre, Paris, France; courtesy the WebMuseum (http://sunsite.unc.edu/wm/) and curator, Nicolas Pioch

Page 107: *The Four Horsemen of the Apocalypse* by Albrecht Dürer; courtesy Carol Gerten-Jackson (http://www.bod.net/Cjackson)

Page 111: *The Four Holy Men* by Albrecht Dürer; Alte Pinakothek, Munich, Germany; courtesy Mark Harden and the texas.net Museum of Art (http://lonestar.texas.net/~mharden)

Page 112: *Knight, Death, & the Devil*, Albrecht Dürer; courtesy Carol Gerten-Jackson (http://www.bod.net/Cjackson)

Page 112: *Self-portrait at 26* by Albrecht Dürer; Museo del Prado, Madrid, Spain; courtesy Corel Photo Library

Page 112: *Self-portrait at 28* by Albrecht Dürer; Alte Pinakothek, Munich, Germany; courtesy the WebMuseum (http://sunsite.unc.edu/wm/) and curator, Nicolas Pioch

Page 113: *Portrait of Zwingli* by Frans Pourbus the Elder; Uffizi, Florence, Italy; courtesy Alinari/Art Resource, NY

Page 119: Zwingli Leaving Zurich, wood engraving, artist unknown, printed in D'Aubigné, History of the Reformation, Putnam & Sons, 1872 (author's collection)

Page 137: *Portrait of Henry VIII*, Hans Holbein the Younger; courtesy Carol Gerten-Jackson (http://www.bod.net/Cjackson)

Page 143: wood engraving of Sir Thomas More, after a portrait by Holbein, artist unknown, printed in D'Aubigné, History of the Reformation, Putnam & Sons, 1872 (author's collection)

Page 147: *Portrait of William Tyndale*, anonymous; Hertford College, Oxford, England; courtesy the Principal and Fellows of Hertford College

Page 149: *Images of Tyndale's New Testament*, courtesy Sandra Elaine Fuentes of The University of Texas at Austin, Graduate School of Library and Information Science (http://www.gslis.utexas.edu/~sefuen/exhibit.html)

Page 154: wood engraving of Cranmer, after an original in the collection at Lambeth Palace, artist unknown, printed in D'Aubigné, History of the Reformation, Putnam & Sons, 1872 (author's collection)

Page 159: *Portrait of John Calvin*, anonymous; Bibliotèque Publique et Universitaire, Geneva, Switzerland; courtesy Tad Crisp

Page 171: *John Knox*; courtesy Image Select/Art Resource, NY

Page 173: *1560 Geneva Bible*, courtesy Thomas Nelson Publishers, Nashville, TN; photograph by Tad Crisp

Colophon

This book was typeset using Quark Xpress, version 3.2. The typeface throughout is a TrueType version of Century Schoolbook, a typeface designed for ease of reading. Our version of this popular font came from Corel.

Original drafts of the manuscript were prepared using Microsoft Word, version 7.0. My grateful thanks to the design team which included such a helpful spelling checker. The Word Grammar Helps were also used extensively, though I did have to turn off the rules on gender-specific nouns. Most of the time "king" and "prince" really are the correct choices!

The illustrations were acquired from several sources. Art Resources in New York City searched their archives and found numerous portraits for us. We used several images from the Corel Photo Library. And we are grateful to the Principal and Fellows of Hertford College in Oxford for permission to use a portion of their portrait of William Tyndale. We would also like to thank Thomas Nelson Publishers of Nashville for allowing us to photograph both their 1560 Geneva Bible and the 1617 King James Bible. Several photographs were supplied by Tad Crisp, Greenleaf's graphic designer in 1996.

We are grateful to Carol Gerten-Jackson and her online Fine Art Gallery at http://www.bod.net/Cjackson. A fortuitous search on the Internet one morning landed us on her pages. By mid-afternoon, we had made an email inquiry, and received her gracious permission to use black & white versions of some of her scans of Renaissance artwork. For those of you with web access, her ever-growing site has hundreds of high-quality color scans of fine artwork. Consider becoming a financial supporter of her online gallery.

Another extremely useful source for art on the Web is the WebMuseum, created by curator Nicolas Pioch. The artwork is mirrored at several sites, but you might start with http://www.sunsite.unc.edu/wm/. We are extremely grateful to Mr. Picoch for permission to use artwork from the WebMuseum.

And finally, our thanks to Mark Harden, who gave us permission to use several scans from his Texas.net Museum of Art. His site can be reached at http://lonestar.texas.net/~mharden.

Our 4-color cover design and the black & white body of the book were output to film from our Quark files and first printed by Darby Printing, Atlanta, GA. We have since converted to .pdf output which goes directly to digital presses without the need for film.

All original design and production software was run under Windows 95 on two ZEOS Pantera PC's with Intel Pentium-90 chips.

CPSIA information can be obtained at www.ICGtesting.com
Printed in the USA
LVOW09s2257010816

498664LV00001B/4/P

9 781882 514106